Unstoppable

THE UNLIKELY **STORY OF A** SILICON VALLEY **GODFATHER**

D1604342

Unstoppable

THE UNLIKELY **STORY OF A** SILICON VALLEY **GODFATHER**

ROY L. CLAY, SR

with M.H. JACKSON

Published in the United States by RLC Publishing, California

Photograph credits: Interior photos courtesy the Clay family archive

Cover Design: Akapo Afeez
Cover Photography: Clay Family Archive, Akapo Afeez
Copy Editing: Erica Young, Joyful Editing

Written by: Roy L. Clay with M. H. Jackson
For information about this book contact us by email at unstoppableroyclay@gmail.com or on Instagram @unstoppableroyclay

The manuscript is based on the life story as told by Roy L. Clay. Information regarding the history and background of Roy L. Clay can be found at https://unstoppableroyclay.com/

ISBN: 978-0-578-26918-4

To my beloved wife, **Virginia Clay**

~**My heart. My soul. My inspiration**~

Contents

INTRODUCTION..1

Chapter One: HUMBLE BEGINNINGS 5

Chapter Two: COMING OF AGE 23

Chapter Three: ALONG CAME VIRGINIA 39

Chapter Four: CALIFORNIA HERE WE COME 59

Chapter Five: OPEN UP THAT GOLDEN GATE.................83

Chapter Six: HP DAYS 103

Chapter Seven: THE DAWN OF "SILICON VALLEY" 121

Chapter Eight: WHEN MY LIFE CHANGED FOREVER 151

Chapter Nine: THEY COULDN'T STOP ME!......................173

Chapter Ten: LOSING VIRGINIA................................197

Chapter Eleven: THIS LIFE GOES ON...........................217

ACKNOWLEDGMENTS 247

INTRODUCTION

It has often crossed my mind how close my life came to an end on a hot summer day in Ferguson, Missouri, a suburb of St. Louis, located just east of my hometown of Kinloch. It was the summer of 1944, following my first year of high school. After working that day as a gardener, I found myself being forcibly handcuffed by police officers and violently thrown into the back seat of their patrol car. The sound of the car door slamming behind me was as much humiliating as it was terrifying. I will never forget the look on the faces of those officers, one of them with a more ominous stare than the other officer who appeared more empathetic. Both men were white, and Ferguson was an all-white town, which made the situation more intimidating for a young black teenager, like me, at that time.

Minutes earlier, I was sitting on a street curb in my overalls and work boots, drinking a cold soft drink and minding my business. Now, I was sweating bullets and feeling that my life was in imminent danger. There was a nauseating smell inside that patrol car which reminded me of cigarette smoke, coffee, and spoiled food; I imagine it was a combination of them all. I remembered that odor for years afterward, along with the sound of the officers' gravelly voices and the shrieking noises coming from the two-way radio that was like something from a bad dream. Unfortunately for me, it was real.

Suddenly, I felt the vehicle moving and glanced, instinctively, out of the window on my right. The route was recognizable as we slowly moved towards Kinloch, stopping at well-spaced stop signs along the way. I noticed a few perfectly manicured lawns that I had just mowed and trimmed earlier that week. The officers were not saying much, and I certainly was not asking any questions. I kept thinking to myself, *what did I do wrong?* After all, when the officers approached me while I was sitting on the street curb in front of a grocery store and asked me what I was doing there, I responded politely. I explained that I was tired from cutting lawns and gardening, so I purchased a cold drink from the store to quench my thirst before heading back home to Kinloch. That is the last thing I remember before being hurled against that vehicle, frisked, cuffed, and locked inside that car, fearing for my life.

I was not the best at praying back then, but this moment brought out prayers I never thought I had inside. We had only driven about a mile and a half. However, that ride seemed to last forever as we finally approached the intersection that crossed into the city of Kinloch. In between trembling and praying, I faintly overheard the more pleasant officer whispering to his partner to just drop me off and let me go. I thought, *could this be my prayers being answered?* The car stopped, and the officers opened their doors. Again, many thoughts were going through my mind, including the fact that a body of water, Bailey's Pond, was located less than a hundred feet away, just below a steep grassy bank lined with shade trees. Growing up, I had always heard of bad things happening to young men in or near that pond, and I was hoping not to be another victim.

I was as frightened as I had ever been in my life, and at that moment, I was envisioning the worst and wondering how I would escape if they tried to take me toward that water. Then I was pulled out of the car, handcuffs removed, and given a stern warning by the more harassing of the two officers. "Nigger, don't let me catch you again in Ferguson; now get on home before I change my mind." Shaking nervously, I walked away afraid but somewhat relieved, thinking about what might have happened if I had made one wrong move, or if the officer with the kind heart had not been on duty that day. It could be said that I was lucky, as some seventy years later, an 18-year-old black man, Michael Brown, Jr, was fatally shot by a white Ferguson police officer not far from where I had fortunately survived my encounter with the Ferguson police.

I did not look back while walking away on that unforgettable day; the distance between those officers and me became lengthier with each step and every gasping breath I took. There was a sigh of relief, however, when I felt myself being beyond the blow of a club or the striking distance of a bullet. I was safe now, on my side of that pond, but without a source of income for the remainder of the summer.

When I arrived home, I told my mother what I had experienced with those white officers in Ferguson. Her first response was, "You did the right thing, Roy. There is no telling what they may have done if you had taken off running or something like that." She went on to say, "You will experience racism for the rest of your life, but don't ever let that be a reason why you don't succeed." Those were words of wisdom I would never forget. She also taught me to "give respect to get respect" and that "education is the key that opens many doors." My mom's advice helped me succeed, no matter the challenges life presented, and I have also instilled the same wisdom in my sons.

There is so much more that I want to share with you about my unlikely journey from a deprived Kinloch, Missouri youth to a successful Silicon Valley pioneer. Come along as we travel the road that is the story of my life.

Chapter One

HUMBLE BEGINNINGS

If you have never heard of Kinloch, Missouri, it is a town with a rich history that includes several unlikely firsts. The first International Air Meet in the United States was held there. The first airmail letter was sent from there, and President Theodore Roosevelt made history when he became the first president to fly in an airplane from right there in St Louis County – "a flight heard around the world," as some say. The town is also considered Missouri's first black city. Thus, the first Black school superintendents and boards of education in the state were rooted in Kinloch. The first time I opened my eyes and breathed some of the earth's fresh midwestern air into my lungs was in Kinloch. It would be my birthplace - where I was raised, nurtured, and instilled with values I would carry with me for a lifetime.

I was born on August 22, 1929, in this small suburb of St. Louis, with a population of fewer than 3,000 residents then. Those residents, who were almost all black, had migrated mostly from the bible belt states, like Alabama,

Mississippi, Arkansas, and other points south. The stock market had taken a record plunge a few months before I was born, a foreshadowing of what would come next. Just two months after my birth, America officially fell helplessly into what would be known as the Great Depression, and it would last well into the mid-1930s. This obviously was not the best of times to be brought into this world, but it wasn't the worst either for a Black child. It was a period in America of immense financial deprivation, but Black Americans didn't have as much to lose, so it slightly leveled the playing field for us, in an ironic kind of way.

Still, it was a struggle for my family as we were also dealing with segregation and not only last hired but also first fired. Former First Lady, Jacqueline Kennedy, was born exactly one month before me that year. Our paths were quite different, however. She was born white, to a prominent Southampton, New York family, who, despite being first generation Americans, were treated as full citizens with all due rights and privileges. My family had helped build this country for generations, but because we faced discrimination solely because of the color of our skin, we did not have equal rights and were still without the freedoms of white Americans. The first lady and I both survived the Great Depression. I beat the odds and became successful as well, but life wasn't as easy for me. So, when I think back over my "wonderful life," it seems that I may have always had some angels guarding and driving me along the way.

My parents, Charles John and Emma Jean Clay, were originally from Alabama but moved to Missouri shortly after they married, partly to look for better opportunities, but mostly because my father's grandparents had a large plot of land in Kinloch that they acquired at the turn of the century. It was enough land to build about three houses. One thing we know is that my mother and father both had parents who were property owners. In the 1920s, my parents and my grandparents moved to Kinloch and built two houses on their family-owned land.

For the first time, masses of Black folks in America were voluntarily relocating and making decisions about their futures, and that took courage. My family was no exception as they moved North and left their cotton-picking days behind them. There was no future in the unskilled and menial work that the Jim Crow South had to offer, so it was time to migrate anywhere but South, as Langston Hughes stated in his classic, 'One Way Ticket.'

> *"I pick up my life*
>
> *And take it with me*
>
> *Any place that is North and East —*
>
> *And not Dixie"*

Those four lines summarize Hughes's thoughts in this piece. It was his opinion that we (Black folks) should be willing to go anywhere but South, on a one-way ticket, to escape the racism and hopelessness of Jim Crow. Once in the North, there was hope for a better life for Black people to provide for their families. Hughes did not publish this poem until 1949, but it was just as relevant to the 1920s for my parents and their contemporaries when they moved to Missouri. They heard stories about the Harlem Renaissance, a Black cultural movement that had begun to take shape in the 1920s. Previously upper middle-class white Harlem had become a mecca for musicians, writers, artists, and black academia's brightest to feel free to express themselves and fulfill their hopes and dreams in ways they had never thought possible before. Soon there were successful Black businesses and opportunities for men and women of color to display and develop their talents and abilities all over Harlem, a community that had taken on a rhythm and heartbeat like no other.

The word got around about the benefits of moving North and becoming successful in places like Harlem, so folks began to pack up and move to the North in record numbers. In the Midwest, cities like Kansas City, Chicago, Detroit, and St Louis were popular destinations for Black people to migrate and make a living. I'm sure my family would have been more interested in the urban charm of St Louis, a city that was dubbed "the gateway to the west" by this time. They got close but settled in little Kinloch; as they say, the rest is history.

I can imagine how excited my parents were to get away from the deep South, but much of Missouri was still segregated. My parents thought they were leaving bigotry and racism behind, but after a while, they realized things were not much different. You see, Missouri entered the Union in 1821 as a slave state following the Missouri Compromise of 1820. In that agreement, Congress decided that slavery would be illegal in all territories north of the 36 degrees, 30 latitude parallel (an imaginary line west of the Mississippi River), except Missouri. That federal legislation was to stop any other attempts from northern territories to be admitted in the future as slave states. As part of the compromise Maine, formally a part of Massachusetts, would be admitted as a free state that same year, restoring the political balance.

Accordingly, Missouri was not in the Deep South, but it was still segregated because of its racially separate past, unlike most states located that far north. Therefore, you could call our town Kinloch, but you might as well have called it deprivation, as the white towns and communities, such as Ferguson, just to the east of us, were much better off than we were, and that's just the way it was in those days.

I was the fourth child born to my parents, and when my mother was finished having children, there were nine siblings altogether. My sisters were Pauline, Myrtle, Imogene, and Hope. My four brothers were Thaddeus, Charles, Buddy, and Haile. There were times when my mother would be feeding a toddler and at the same time trying to figure out how to help pay her oldest child's college tuition. Mothering suited her, and it was apparent that she and my father enjoyed family life.

They were significant role models and the best providers they could be, considering the daily disparities and struggles they had to overcome. I never had to look outside for mentoring and guidance because it was right there in our home. As far back as I remember, we were taught to respect each other, and it was established that the oldest child in the household, at any given time, was to be the leader when our parents were not at home. We learned the importance of family and that we should also protect and support each other outside of the household. After all these years, I still think about how my next older brother, Charles, supported me to the end of whatever I pursued. He was my protector, for sure.

I am told that Kinloch was originally Kinloch Park, developed in the 1890s as a commuter town for whites located about 5 miles west of St. Louis. A small part of the land was reserved for Black people (or negroes as we were called in those days) who came to work there as servants. Rumor has it that the Black migration to Kinloch started when a certain black woman and her husband bought a piece of land through their friendship with a fair-minded white homeowner. When their white neighbors discovered the new owners were Black, they quickly sold their properties and moved. As a result, no other white families would move into a large section of the community. That left white property owners one option: allow Black people to purchase those available lots. Black people would eventually take over the entire southeast portion of the community, the same community that would later be named South Kinloch.

An early version of the classic "white flight" had taken place. Some whites remained in a small area of Kinloch Park, but eventually, all parts of the area were owned or rented by Black people; thus, Kinloch, the little black city, was born.

Make no mistake, Kinloch was a small town when my parents and grandparents moved there, settled down, and grew our family. We are not sure how my grandfather was able to purchase the land, but my great-grandfather, Jesse Shelton, was a respected landowner and one of the first Black men to vote in Sumpter County, Alabama, during Reconstruction. As it often happens with facts about the history of Black families, we are not sure how he acquired that large amount of land (about 300 acres) in Alabama, but it sure made a difference in our lives. Records show that Jesse was literate and owned property, so he was eligible to vote in 1868 and 1870 in the local and national elections. However, we don't know what eventually happened to that land he owned in Alabama. It's as if it vanished as strangely as it was acquired.

It was evident we came from *good stock* though, as the old folks would say, and I'm sure that had a lot to do with my family owning property in Kinloch years after our ancestor Jesse Shelton had shown us that it was possible.

Kinloch was a rural place in so many ways. Most folks grew their own vegetables and even had fruit trees in their yards. Quite a few of the residents raised chickens as well. The houses were typically small, grayish-colored frame houses, as in most working-class Black communities. Some had porches lined with colorful potted flowers that many neighboring women claimed for bragging rights during the summer months. Our house was a one-level gray framed home that, in later years, always seemed to need a fresh coat of paint for some reason. There was a large basement level with a back entrance from a downward sloping backyard. This is where the boy's bedroom was located. We did not have a front porch. My grandparents lived next door, and their house was similar, except it had a porch that stretched across the front of the house, with railings full of exotic-looking plants in the summer that were taken inside during the chilly winter months. Only a handful of the families owned cars initially, but by the time I reached my late teens, there were a few more car owners driving on those dusty roads. Just imagine a town with no streetlights, no sewer system, no sidewalks, and only about five paved roads in town. That was Kinloch.

We lived on Carson Road, one of the busiest streets in town back then and one of the few paved ones. It was a main thoroughfare. Many of the businesses in town were situated on or near Carson Road, so the heartbeat and soul of Kinloch was ever visible and heard along that busy asphalt paved road. The unrestrained bursts of laughter from children at play, the thud of a baseball into a catcher's mitt, the crack of a bat, a neighbor pushing a lawn mower or sawing timber for firewood, the noisy yet familiar sounds of box trucks delivering ice to residential homes and occasional delivery trucks bringing weekly supplies to the business establishments like clockwork. Then there was the occasional rumble of an automobile slowly driving through with frequent honks of the distinctive sounding horns of those times, sometimes for warning but most times just for greeting. It was comfortable on that old street though, because we were part of it - that was our life. Segregated conditions had so many negatives, especially with us being on the unequal side of things. Still, there was an upside to living in a Black town. There were genuine opportunities for Black businesses to succeed, which amazed me.

A couple of small stores had everything, including hardware, gardening supplies, and flowers. One of the stores was more like a five-and-dime store and carried over-the-counter medicines. There were two or three barbershops and hair salons, three churches, and of course, a pool hall – and there was nothing you couldn't find there, which I found out later as a teenager. There were carpenters, bricklayers, house painters, and a few hustlers as well. I'll just call them "butlers" for now. One thing about it, in poor neighborhoods like this, there were always more people than there were jobs, especially during the Great Depression era. Understandably so, some folks had to be a bit creative. Sometimes they had to do things they had to do, which were often not what they wanted to do, to feed their families and survive – and that's what it was like for many of the men in Black communities with little resources. It was about survival.

There was nothing that you needed that somebody in Kinloch could not find for you or do for you. Everybody knew one another, and we all knew who to contact to get things done, and that was a good thing. As a kid growing up, I always thought Black folks had a certain business sense or enterprising spirit. Someone was always going door to door, sitting in front of the store, or standing on the corner intending to sell something. I'm not sure how much they sold, but they were always there, so that was impressive to me, and my guess is they made enough to get by.

We were on the east side of town, just before you would reach the city of Ferguson, Missouri. Though both sides of our street (Carson Road) were in the town of Kinloch, the west side was in the Kinloch school district, and the east side was oddly within the Ferguson school district. Since our house was on the east side of the road, I went to school in Ferguson.

The Ferguson school district was racially segregated, but in 1928, they built a two-room schoolhouse for Black students. It was named Vernon School. There was a downstairs classroom that accommodated the kindergarten to fourth-grade level students. The upstairs classroom was used to accommodate the fifth through eighth-grade students. Both classrooms looked much the same. They had large windows on two sides, with a spacious cloakroom. They were furnished with small one-armed desks, all righthanded, so not so good for the few lefthanded students who attended at the time. The wooden floors were shiny and clean most of the time, and the walls were an egg-shell color. We had black chalkboards in both rooms, and boy did I like volunteering to clean those chalkboards – sometimes that was worth an extra milk at recess.

Ms. Viola Clay (no relation) was my K through 4th-grade teacher. She had been there since the school opened, but she was a relatively young woman. I thought she was so nice and very pretty. She was a small woman, with a light complexion and shoulder-length deep brown hair. Ms. Adele Harris was my fifth through eighth-grade teacher. She was a petite woman as well. Both of these ladies wore small-framed reading glasses and dressed professionally. If Hollywood agents were casting a schoolteacher for a 1930s movie, either of those ladies would have fit the part.

The school enrolled only forty students. They had to have a school for negro children in Ferguson because it was a segregated school district. Since only a hand full of blacks lived in Ferguson, mostly servants to the middle-class whites, they figured out a way to assign children from that one street in Kinloch to meet the numbers they needed to keep that school open. The school in Kinloch was much older, with fewer resources. I was fortunate to be assigned to the school in Ferguson. It was not equal to the white school, but it was a better learning environment than the school in the Kinloch district. Throughout my school years at Vernon, the emphasis was on reading, writing, oral communication, and arithmetic. When I graduated from elementary school, my understanding of numbers, vocabulary, and writing skills were well above average. That helped prepare me to be a better student in high school and college.

My father worked in building maintenance for Wagner Electric Company in Wellston, Missouri, St Louis County, for his entire career. The skills he acquired at Wagner Electric enabled him to help build, improve and maintain our home. He was a diligent worker and took his job seriously. He was also very likable and a natural leader. I admired that about him. My mother was a housewife, managing the day-to-day responsibilities of our home and providing for my eight siblings and me. She also became a seamstress, making clothes for our family and serving the community.

My mother learned the seamstress skills while taking home economics classes when she attended a small historically black college (HBCU) in Alabama, before marrying my father and moving north. She was a brilliant woman and served as president of the Parents Teachers Association (PTA) the entire time I attended Vernon Elementary School.

My mother and father were devout members of the Baptist church, and my father became an assistant pastor of the local church. My mother instilled in me that education should be my highest priority. She would say, "With education, you will own something that can't be taken from you, and you will be in possession of something that will lead you to life success; with it, you have a chance for success, without it you will be lucky to succeed." She prepared me for school by having my clothes ready and breakfast prepared. She was always at home when I arrived from school. I would ask if I could go out to play, and I was expected home at dark. My parents were not harsh with discipline. However, they would inform me when they thought I had done something wrong. It was uncanny how good they were at parenting. Even when they occasionally disagreed, they managed it discreetly and never disagreed with each other in my presence.

My mother instilled in me that I should do the best I could - no more, but no less. I quickly realized that she thought I was extremely bright. She would review my report cards, and if I received any grade less than excellent, she would ask, "Do you have a problem with this subject?" I would simply say "no" and make sure to get excellent grades after that. The underlying message was to always perform to the best of my ability. I was to learn as much as I could, about everything that I could, as rapidly as I could.

Equally important, I was taught to do what is morally and ethically right. I learned that one must give respect in order to receive respect. Therefore, I still give respect, and I appreciate receiving respect in return. If respect is not returned, I ask myself if it matters. If it doesn't matter, then I just walk away. If it matters that I didn't get respect in return, then I determine how I can get through it or around it. The Kinloch street jargon was "for your respect, I respect you, for your disrespect, forget you." A four-letter word was substituted for the word "forget" most times. In summary, I have always learned as much as I can, tried to do the right thing, and given respect to earn respect.

We had little money, but I never felt poor. I was taught that not having money is a temporary condition in a person's life, whereas being poor is a state of mind. Call me Abe Lincoln if you like, but I studied by candlelight until my father was able to bring electricity inside the house. He was very industrious and learned that from watching others while working at the electric company. He also worked to get plumbing in the house for several years, and by the time I was about twelve, we had running water and a toilet. From then on, it was no more outhouse and washtub for the Clays. My mother would say, "Cleanliness is next to godliness." That meant it was bathing time, which happened more often once we got that plumbing done.

We ate in a kitchen on the main level of the house at a fixed time for the entire family for breakfast, lunch, and dinner. There was a dining room reserved for Sunday and holiday dining. The food we ate was almost always from our family garden. My father learned his gardening skills in Alabama and passed them on to us. We planted kale, collards, beans, corn, tomatoes, cucumbers – you name it. Mother regularly canned and preserved products from the garden and prepared them for dinner year-round. Her canning skills were second to none. My favorite foods were my mother's corn, which she always made taste better than anyone else, and her special fried chicken. I loved buttermilk as a child as well. There was a living room reserved for guests' visits and for displaying photographs to honor African Americans, like Frederick Douglass, George Washington Carver, Charles Drew, and others.

Above all, my mother was an expert seamstress who made most of my clothes. You would have to go to St. Louis to find clothing as nice as what Mother could make. She made extra money for the family with her seamstress business, which was a blessing. Back then, Black schools were big on teaching trades and skills like that, especially in Alabama, where Booker T. Washington made it so important at Tuskegee Institute. Since my mother was so good at making our clothes, the first commercially made suit I owned was purchased for my high school graduation when I was seventeen. We never owned an automobile during that time, so we traveled by public transportation or by walking. This was typical of many Black families in our community. An automobile was a luxury.

When I entered kindergarten at five years of age, and ever since I can remember, I knew I was expected to go to college. After my older sister, Pauline, entered Lincoln University, an HBCU in Jefferson City, Missouri, my mother would take me along in transporting my sister to and from the campus. I also went to Lincoln for annual homecomings. From those experiences, I envisioned college ultimately being my future, and while in grade school and high school, I felt anxious to get there. Therefore, starting in kindergarten and throughout my childhood, I always visualized attending college. It was clear that there would be no alternative.

My parents, Charles and Emma Jean Clay at their 25th Anniversary celebration

Me and my siblings with our parents in the 1930's.

Chapter Two

COMING OF AGE

November 3, 1939 was a life-changing date for me. A neighbor, James Roby, had asked my mother to let me live with him and his family. They had given me clothes to wear and served me dinner at their home. Mr. Roby picked up and hauled trash for a living and did better financially than most in Kinloch. I was only a kid, but he invited me to work with him. I enjoyed the work and was paid a small sum of money to do so. He would tell me that he could teach me to make a living by hustling, a word often heard back in the day. My mother approved the move, which was scheduled to take effect on Friday, November 3, 1939, as it would not only benefit Mr. Roby, but it would be more money for our family. I dreaded the decision and lost nights of sleep over it. Mr. Roby felt it would be a relief for my parents as they struggled to raise nine children. However, I loved being around my siblings, day and night, even though there were nine children and two parents, totaling 11 people with only three bedrooms. The boys slept in a bedroom on the basement level. The girls slept in a bedroom on the main level near our parent's bedroom. We ate meals together, we played together, and I absolutely did not want to live with anyone other than my family. Still, there I was, preparing to live with Mr. Roby.

This was when the life-changing incident occurred. I loved sports of all kinds: baseball, boxing, football, and table tennis. On that day in 1939, I was seriously injured playing sandlot football, which affected my sports life forever. Since I was one of the younger guys playing football, I normally did not get my number called, but on this horrific day, I got the ball. They called a *47 sweep on two*. Football was basically a running game then, so the tailback handed off to me as I ran left and was looking to get outside and use my speed, being that I was the smallest guy on the field. However, a defender was right there waiting for me, so I cut back in towards the middle of the field, and that's when it happened. Before I knew it, I was hit by what felt like a Mack truck from my right side. My big brother, Charles, said it was June Thomas, a kid who weighed about 250 pounds. I was right about what hit me; June's nickname was "Truck."

In one fleeting moment, I ran smack into the biggest guy on the field. I suffered a severe injury that included a dislocated pelvis, a compound fracture of my upper leg, a dislocated knee, and a fractured ankle. The accident was compounded because the other guys thought I was faking the injury, and they forced me to stand up and walk or run. All I could think was *who or what hit me?* The pain was so unbearable that I collapsed back to the ground after trying to walk, forcing the guys to realize the severity of the injury. Charles ran home and got my father, who called for an ambulance. It appeared that everything was in slow motion, but I vaguely remember all the guys dropping to one knee and forming a circle around me, protectively, as they waited for help to come. That included Truck Thomas, who I'm told didn't suffer as much as a scratch on that play, but I hear the big fellow shed a tear and said a few prayers for me as I was put on a stretcher and driven away to the hospital by ambulance. That was the longest ride imaginable, at least up until that point in my life.

Once I reached the hospital in St. Louis, my leg was placed in a sling with weights attached to keep the fractured bone together. My mother and father were there fighting back tears for the first couple of days I was there. It was hard for them because they didn't own a car, and St. Louis was a bit of a commute from Kinloch. One day when I was alone at the hospital, an earthquake occurred not too far away on the Madrid fault line. It caused the weights on my leg to swing violently, causing excruciating pain to my body. Luckily, there was a nurse nearby who took good care of me. I was later placed in a body cast which started at my waist, went down my entire right leg, and down to my knee on the left leg. I could not sit up, so I lay prone in the hospital bed. I remained in that position for six weeks. People seemed empathetic when they saw me lying there that way. One day after school, my next older brother, Charles, came to visit me and fainted when he entered my hospital room and saw me in that position. He was a big strong guy, but it must have been extremely difficult for anyone to see me like that, much less for a twelve-year-old like Charles to comprehend it. From that point on, he became protective of me.

I was released to go home after four weeks, but I had to be taken by stretcher and remained in that rigged-up position for two more weeks. Dr. Roy Johnson of Ferguson, Missouri, the doctor who delivered me when I was born, was there on my first day back home to make sure everything was set up right. He returned a week later to check on me. Dr. Johnson was white. Yes, a white doctor delivered me, and that did not happen often during segregation. He was a kind person, like several others who lived in the area, and he had a kind heart. It was always nice when Dr. Johnson made a house call. He smiled and encouraged me, so I always felt a little better when he was there. My mother said that I was named "Roy" after Dr. Johnson, because she and my father always admired him for the way he lived his life. He was always a friend to our family.

My mother was my nurse while I was at home. She was like an angel, caring for me and cautiously feeding me by straw. She also kept a bedpan available because I could not sit upright. My whole family was so caring and attentive during those two weeks, and I was starting to like all the attention. When my mother had to leave out, my siblings were right there by my side, waiting on me. My teacher sent books to read and homework I could complete whenever the pain would subdue enough for me to focus on schoolwork.

After those two weeks, I was taken back to the hospital by ambulance. The body cast was replaced by a cast on my right side. When the body cast was removed, I was asked to sit upright. I fainted when I attempted to do so because I had no strength after lying in that position for six weeks.

I learned to stand and then walk with crutches, one miserable step at a time. Every movement of my body was painful, but I was determined. There were times when I cried at that hospital when no one was around, but after I returned home, my sisters and brothers pushed me and challenged me with a bit of love thrown in there as well. My mother reminded me that I needed to get back to school to avoid being retained in the 5th grade. That really woke me up. Not passing to the 6th grade would have made matters even worse. It was tough, but I had to do it. I just had to physically get back in school.

Two weeks after the body cast was removed, I was able to make my way up the schoolhouse stairs with the help of my crutches, my brother, Charles, and sheer determination. That old classroom was a beautiful sight to see, and as I slowly hobbled to my seat, there was a cheer that got louder with every step I took. Then I noticed that all my classmates were standing, led by my teacher, Miss Harris. The applause lasted several minutes. I cried with joy, and that's the only time I ever cried in school. Miss Harris had baked a cake to celebrate my return, and she remembered that chocolate was my favorite. The kids stared at me a lot for the next couple of weeks and asked me many questions, but it didn't bother me too much because I knew they were probably as amazed as I was that I returned to Vernon School so soon. It was an accomplishment to be back in school, and although I would never be the same athlete as I had been before that devastating injury, it was good to see my classmates. By the grace of God and the help of some angels, I was still alive and on my feet again.

After a four-month absence from school, I was back performing as normal, with no loss of grade level. I began to realize that I was still smart, and I was even more driven to succeed in the classroom, despite the physical injuries. I still get emotional when I think of the first day I entered the classroom, welcomed by a resounding cheer after my long absence and the grueling rehabilitation work I endured. The warmth and love I felt from my classmates and teacher meant the world to me. I felt like my old self again, and I did not want to let them down. From that day forward, I was committed to meeting every challenge. I did all my assignments, finished my required homework, took the final tests, and proceeded to the sixth grade without delay.

When I reached the sixth grade, I was asked to tutor students in arithmetic, students who were at a fifth-grade level. When fifth-grade students performed arithmetic tests, the teacher often asked me to stay after school to grade the tests. My teachers gave me such personal attention that when I graduated from the eighth grade, I firmly believed I could learn anything. Learning had become a natural thing, and more importantly, it was fun. Classwork and studying took my mind off that terrible injury and gave me confidence, which boosted my self-esteem.

World War II started when I was in the seventh grade, and it was a little scary for me as a child. I saw young men leaving Kinloch and going off to fight for Uncle Sam, although old Jim Crow was our enemy at home. I'm not sure if I could have been that patriotic. The U.S. Armed Forces were still segregated, but white America still expected us to pitch in. We went over in big numbers, but I was glad my father didn't have to go, and I was glad I was not old enough at the time. The war went on for several years and continued throughout my time in high school. The closest Black high school I could attend was in Webster Groves, Missouri, approximately forty miles away and a one-hour drive by public transportation. That was the white-folks way to keep us from getting an education, but that didn't work when you came from a family that put education first. No matter how difficult they made it, we were determined to get that diploma. It was an adventure every day, and I couldn't help but notice how different my high school was compared to my elementary school, which was merely a short walk away. It was a totally new environment, with new and exciting challenges. There were 40 students in the entire Vernon school, but at Douglas High, there were 50 students in my freshman class alone.

I gradually grew accustomed to the new environment and performed as well as I could, despite a few setbacks. I always had a little bit of hustler in me and thought I could outsmart almost anyone with my math and thinking abilities. That got me in trouble during my freshman year, as a teacher caught me shooting dice in the gymnasium. It was reported to the school principal, Mr. Goins, and the teacher requested disciplinary action. I suspect that the teacher had profiled me because I was from Kinloch, considered the lowest class community that fed into Douglas High. As a result of the incident, I could have been suspended or expelled, but the principal declined to take action that day. He didn't even contact my parents, and I never told them either.

It's interesting that the student with whom I was shooting craps, Alphonse "Al" Smith, was a great Douglas High School athlete, and was later signed by the Cleveland Indians Baseball Team. He was among the first Blacks to play Major League Baseball after a couple of years in the Negro Leagues. He came to Cleveland and joined Larry Doby, the first black player in the American League. Smith was later named one of the 100 greatest Indians players. I would say that the principal was probably trying to protect his star athlete, Alphonse, who was caught that day in the crap-shooting incident, so he had no choice but to take no action with me as well.

Although the principal took no disciplinary action, I paid a high price for participating in that crap game. It just so happened that the husband of the teacher who observed and reported the incident was also a teacher at the school. I ended up a student in one or both of their classes each of my four years at Douglas. Those two teachers taught me a lesson by making it hard for me in their respective classes. I just barely got by with passing grades in their classes, while I earned the highest possible grade in all my other classes.

The summer after my freshman year at Douglas, I decided to work as a gardener in Ferguson, the town next door. It was an all-white town and was segregated. I knew they needed folks to cut their lawns and trim their hedges, so I went for it. That is when I had the altercation with the two Ferguson City police officers I described in the introduction. I was so frightened that day as those white policemen terrorized me. Imagine being handcuffed and brutally thrown into the back of a police car for no reason other than being black in a white neighborhood a month before your 15th birthday. Fortunately, I survived my encounter with the Ferguson police. I was scared, shaken, and humiliated, but I lived to tell the story.

However, there is a great deal to be said that so many years later, a young man with so much life ahead, was not so lucky. Michael Brown, another young man from Missouri, will not have the opportunity that I had to attend college, build a career, raise a family, and contribute meaningfully to society. All he ever would have been was taken away instantly, for no legitimate reason other than walking down the street while being black. And it all happened right there in Ferguson, the same place where my life was spared some seventy years earlier. It is a memory that will always be there, reminding me how fragile life can be and how fortunate I was to walk away from that experience alive. My life could have vanished in an instant, but the good Lord had other plans for me. He had heard my mother's daily prayers and watched over Emma Jean Clay's son that day. Early on, I learned there was a difference between being black and white in America, but it made me want to prove myself even more. I never went back to work in Ferguson, though – I guess I did not want to press my luck.

One positive thing about doing that gardening work was gaining confidence in my physical abilities again. I wasn't the same as before the injury I suffered at ten, but I was about 16 years old and had healed enough to play baseball again. I loved the game, so my older brothers encouraged me to organize a team, and my brother, Charles, played on the team with me.

All the black towns had ball teams back then, and I played nearly every Sunday. I missed church often because of those Sunday games, but my father was a fan, so he permitted me to play. We had some extremely competitive and entertaining games back then, and my father would sneak out of church to catch a few games himself. World War II was winding down by this time, and since many of the guys I played with were older than me, a few were just returning from overseas. That war took its toll on our young men during the 1940s, and there were a few boys from Kinloch who never made it back to Missouri. It was sad not seeing them again, but they were heroes to us, and we dedicated many of our games to them. The games were exciting, and I remember some of the players we played against moving on to the Negro Leagues. That was fascinating to me as I idolized the players in that league. I had heard of Satchel Paige, Josh Gibson, and Cool Papa Bell. They were my favorites, and in my opinion, they were three of the best ball players who ever walked this earth.

As a youngster, I always aspired to play professional baseball, possibly with the St Louis Cardinals, but most likely with a Negro League team, such as the Kansas City Monarchs, in part because the color line had not been broken yet. However, after that injury I suffered when I was ten years of age, I had little hope of a professional career. Besides, I was relatively small in stature for an athlete, weighing no more than 130 pounds. I played third base for our team without committing an error the whole first season. We were playing only black teams, but there was this one time that we were invited to play a white-only team in Ferguson, Missouri. During a tense moment in that game, a white player attempted to steal third base, but my catcher, Harold, made a perfect throw which I caught, and with one continuous, swiping motion, I tagged the player as he attempted a head-first slide. It was a hard tag to the side of his head as he reached for the bag and caused the player to lose consciousness momentarily. It was a completely innocent play, but the white fans on the other side were outraged at what they felt was an unsportsmanlike act by me. My brother, Charles, rushed toward me from his shortstop position to ensure that no harm would come to me. The ball game was interrupted, and my team was asked to leave the area immediately for fear of a physical confrontation. If you ask me, I think that fellow's feelings were hurt more than anything that afternoon. I heard it was the first time he had been thrown out all season, so being cut down by a black catcher was reason enough for him to lose consciousness and his memory too, I suppose. We boarded our transportation vehicle and left as quickly as we could - with our memories intact but knowing that would most likely be our last time playing in a racially integrated game for a while.

Two years later, we were still playing baseball and following professional ball teams, especially after our star athlete, Alphonse, was signed to a Negro league team. We thought it would only be a matter of time before he would be playing in the majors. Charles had been in the Army for a couple of years by this time, as he had volunteered as soon as he graduated from high school, which was towards the end of World War II. It was about this time that we heard that a black player had broken the color line and was playing with the Brooklyn Dodgers. That player, of course, was Jackie Robinson. There was so much excitement and pride in knowing there was a black player in the majors. Although the Dodgers were scheduled to come to St. Louis to play against the Cardinals, we didn't get a chance to see Jackie play. This was because the Cardinals threatened to strike rather than play that home series against the Dodgers, which caused the already racially divided city to postpone those games, fearing danger to Robinson and black fans. Remember, there were no other teams in the South or playing in a former segregated state other than the Washington Senators, and they were in the American League. They didn't have to play the Dodgers, who were in the National League. We were disappointed, but Major League Baseball's color line had been broken, and that would open the door for more black players in the future.

My friend, Alphonse, who was initially signed to a minor league contract with the Cleveland Indians, eventually went on to play for three other teams during his career. Al became famous for an incident that occurred when he was playing left field for the Chicago White Sox in the 1959 World Series. In what was lauded as one of the favorite World Series moments ever, there was a long fly ball to left field at Comiskey Park. Al backed up to the wall attempting to reach up and catch the ball, but a cup filled with beer was sitting on the rail at the top of that wall. The fan, who sat it there, reached out to catch the ball as it sailed into the seats and he accidentally knocked the cup over. Not only did Al not catch the ball, but the beer poured down onto his head. It was a home run for the Dodgers, and that picture is probably hanging in the Baseball Hall of Fame for sure. If you're scoring the incident, it was one hit, one run, one "social" error, and nothing left in the cup. Oh well, Al always did enjoy a good cold beer back in the neighborhood.

The remainder of my high school days, I earned money working at a popular pool hall in town. It was only a couple blocks from home, and I only worked part-time so I could concentrate on my schoolwork. It was tucked away on a corner at the end of one of our main streets and even had a small parking lot. The building was well maintained outside and bright and well-lit on the inside. It was not smokey either, as there was no smoking allowed inside. The hall had nine pool tables, and it was my job to rack balls and keep the pool hall neat and organized. We also had a small kitchen and served some of the best soul food in town. Occasionally, he had pig feet or chitlin's on the menu, and I would make sure to get a plate to go at the end of the day. I still think about that soul food back home, even today. After working there for about six months, I was asked by the owner to manage the dice game in the back. He had become aware of my math skills in the pool hall and had probably tested my honesty, so he knew he could trust me. I was honored that he thought so highly of me. The patrons in that dice room got a little chippy at times, but I was never afraid. I always knew my big brother, Charles, was well respected and could handle it for me - and there were times that he did.

One particularly chilling incident happened one evening when the owner had stepped out for a moment. There was an argument in the back room, and one of the dice players, Big Jake, accused me of siding with another player and cheating him out of the money he should have won. In a matter of seconds, some guys ran out to the main hall, and there was a hush that came over that back room where we just stared at each other like the O.K. Corral scene in that Wyatt Earp western flick. He kept his eye on me, and I didn't take my eyes off him either —I was so scared I could hardly breathe. I thought to myself, *now how will I get out of this mess?* I had no chance because this grown man, easily in his mid-twenties, had the barrel of a gun pointed at my head. My only weapon was that pen and notebook pad I used to calculate the dice winnings. Where was *Doc Holiday* when I needed him? All of a sudden, the guy puts his gun away and mumbles something about me not being worth it; then, over that mumble I hear a strong, familiar voice behind me. "Relax, Roy. He won't bother you anymore. It was just a misunderstanding, right Jake?" It was my big brother, Charles, who had been playing pool out front. He had my back and may have saved my life that night. Jake walked away that night with a certain fear I had not witnessed in him before. Even when Jake returned to roll dice in the back room in the future, he always had a certain respect for me after that run-in with Charles. Even the tough guys in town didn't mess with my big brother. Whatever Charles had, I wanted some, but I settled for Charles being there for me, protecting me, and always having my back.

The pool hall owner, who I called Deacon, was the most popular businessman in town and had other businesses, including a grocery store. He was a small, sharp-featured, quiet man, who just took care of business. I learned leadership skills by watching and admiring how he managed things. He had children about my age, and they helped him with his other businesses. He would often ask me about my grades in school to ensure I was staying on the right path. He said he wanted me to get a college degree and leave Kinloch someday. He was my first true example of a successful black businessman; he inspired me to believe I could be like him someday. That pool hall is also how I made money while attending St. Louis University, but it all started from working there while I was in high school.

I didn't date much in high school, although I had met a few nice girls in my classes. I talked to them after school and helped them with their schoolwork, but I was just so focused on playing baseball, working at the pool hall, and finishing first in my class that I didn't really have time for much else. I was able to manage my workload very well, between school and my job at the pool hall. I was determined to succeed and knew I would make it if I followed my parents' advice. I disappointed them when I received less than stellar grades from the two teachers who made my studies miserable because of the crap game I was caught participating in during high school. As a result, my overall grade point average (GPA) ended up being only a 3.91 instead of 4.0. What made it worst was that the valedictorian's GPA was 3.92. However, my class standing still earned me an academic scholarship to St Louis University. All the other schools of higher education were still segregated in Missouri, but SLU was a Jesuit school, and they made a moral decision to accept all people regardless of their race, religion, or creed. So, there I was, a black kid from little deprived Kinloch, about to be one of the first black students to be accepted to a very prestigious, previously whites-only University. Now, it was time to show the world that I could compete anywhere.

Chapter Three

ALONG CAME VIRGINIA

T o say I was excited about going to college would be an understatement. My transition from high school to the highly esteemed St. Louis University (SLU) presented a brand-new life for me. It was a stark contrast to what I had experienced in Kinloch. The sprawling campus with many buildings – which were exceptionally large structures with enormous classrooms and lecture halls, would provide new academic and cultural challenges. This new life consisted of a racially integrated learning environment with white leadership only. I had never experienced racism in my prior educational background because the students, faculty, and administrators were all black.

I had dealt with segregation, but school always felt safe and welcoming until I landed at dear old SLU. It wasn't old Jim Crow, but the subtle and systemic racism was often prevalent. What came to my mind quickly that first semester was the statement my mother made after that nearly disastrous altercation I had as a teenager with those

Ferguson police officers. My mother's advice that I should "be prepared to encounter racism for the rest of my life, but never let that be a reason that I don't succeed" seemed to be in my thoughts during my first days at SLU.

I was always highly competitive in the classroom. Without those excellent grades in high school, I would not have been accepted to St. Louis University. However, there was another significant reason why I was able to be considered for that scholarship. Missouri was still a segregated state, just as the other former slave states were at that time. Prior to 1946, in keeping with the policies of the state, St. Louis University, a prestigious Jesuit institution, and the first university established west of the Mississippi River, did not admit black students.

As if heaven-sent, Father Claude Heithaus, S.J., of SLU delivered a powerful sermon at the College Church located on the university campus in 1944, which denounced racial prejudice in America. This started a dialogue among clergy and lay people alike and eventually led to the integration of St. Louis University. Later that summer, two black undergraduates and three black graduate students were admitted to the university, making it the first university in a former slave state to establish an official policy for integration.

So, it came to pass that a few more black students were admitted to the SLU in the next two years, and I was one of them. With Father Heithaus and St. Louis University leading the way for equal justice at the higher education level, Archbishop Joseph E. Ritter became the new leader of the Archdiocese of St. Louis in 1946. One of Archbishop Ritter's first orders was to instruct all pastors in the archdiocese to end racial segregation in the city's parochial schools. In 1947, St. Louis parochial schools were notified that they must include black children or face religious discipline. The U. S. Supreme Court would not take the same action with the nation's public schools until 1954, but here I was in the middle of the integration of the St. Louis archdiocese and St. Louis University. The archbishop was serious about this new policy and warned that any staff members, priests, or parishioners who protested would be excommunicated from the church, so there was little resistance or protesting. The handful of black students, including myself, did not come from wealthy backgrounds, so the only way this desegregation policy would work was if there would be scholarship money available for us. Thank goodness it was offered, and I quickly accepted before they had a chance to change their minds. Archbishop Ritter was widely praised. He was recognized in St. Louis and throughout the United States. He said he saw the decision as a simple matter of justice.

My college life and new environment was like nothing I had experienced before. There were no fraternities that accepted blacks and no invitations to join clubs. The student housing and dormitories were not accommodating to us either. Therefore, I lived at home and commuted to the campus on public transportation, making sure I was seated in the back, of course. I was always dressed well getting on that bus, thanks to my mother's seamstress skills. I had a nice collection of pullover vests, crewneck sweaters, and gaberdine slacks. I wore a black brimmed hat with a white hatband during the fall and winter seasons, and my shoes were always shined. My favorite shirt was a black and white gaucho shirt that I purchased with money from my job at the pool hall. That shirt went well with my hat. It was a casual look, but by today's standards, I was dressed up. By the time I was a senior, t-shirts had become popular, so I had two or three that I wore often. I was easily noticeable in the classrooms on campus, not because of my clothing style but because I was always the only black person in the class.

I had entered a world made for and run by White America. It was a divided city, just like most of our nation, so how would I be able to make it? The theatre on Grand Avenue, across from the campus, was for whites only. All the local restaurants served *Whites Only,* and that, unfortunately, included a couple of restaurants that were located on the university-owned property as well.

On one occasion, I ignored the whites-only restriction and sat in an off-campus restaurant. While I was reading the menu and waiting for service, the manager came to me and said rather politely, "I am very sorry, but our guests do not wish for you to be served." Can you imagine being an 18-year-old college freshman, all alone, hearing those words for the first time? I looked around the room for a friend, and there were no faces that looked like mine and no faces that sympathized with me. Those stoic stares were grim and unfriendly, so my initial thought to smile politely, remain seated at that table, and place an order vanished as swiftly as it came into my mind. Now, with no friends, or my big brother, Charles, there to back me up, I promptly left that restaurant without a whisper, looking over my shoulder and making sure I wasn't followed on the way out. I knew if there was trouble, I might be suspended from SLU, and that was the last thing I needed. This was another experience that can take the pride away from a man, but it just gave me more motivation to work harder and prove myself even more. I was committed to succeeding, and maybe then I could be an advocate for justice, even if only by example.

The faculty and many of the students were still a little uncomfortable with this integration thing. As a matter of fact, it was new to all of us. In my first semester, there was an incident where the professor announced over the public address system that he felt that the student who made the highest score on a recent examination had done so by cheating. I learned later that I was the student to whom he was referring. I wrote a paper for my English class entitled "The Purpose of Education." I received an excellent grade for the paper, but the professor did not believe I had the ability to write that well, so he asked who helped me write it. I told him I never cheated and that I had always completed my own work. He accepted the paper, although I am not sure he ever believed me, that is, until the end of the semester when I finished with the highest score in the class. This same thing happened again when I wrote a paper for my German class, in German. Again, another professor accused me of getting someone to write it. Whereas I was considered among the brightest throughout my educational experience in a segregated environment growing up, I was not thought of as bright enough to succeed on my own by the faculty at St. Louis University.

Unfortunately, that was what I had to live with for the next four years, without mentors and with only a handful of students who were similarly situated. That was the environment, and even though it was stressful and unfair, I again referred to my mother's statement, "You will meet racism for the rest of your life, but don't ever let that be the reason that you don't succeed."

It was not all bad at SLU. At times, the university environment included elements of fun and enjoyment. For instance, there was a Jesuit priest who occasionally joined my monthly Saturday night poker party, which often lasted until daybreak. He was glad to hear about our little card-playing festivities and blended in like one of the guys. Man, did he enjoy the St. Louis style ribs and fried chicken that was always on hand. Sometimes I think he enjoyed the food as much as he liked the card games. One thing we knew is that when Father was playing, that was one less person we had to worry about cheating. All he had to do was say a few Hail Marys under his breath, and the good Lord seemed to send him the winning hand. I began to try it myself, but for some reason, it never worked for me. I hope he didn't have an early mass on those Sunday mornings, after those card-playing nights, because he was always one of the last guys to leave. This young poker-playing priest also happened to be the moderator during my oracle examination one year, wherein, I chose matrix mathematics as my area of special interest and I did okay - Thanks Father.

Out of the handful or so of black students I knew, there was one other student who was dealing with some of the same issues as me; I befriended him from the start. That student was Robert Williams, a native of St. Louis. We tried our best to help each other cope with being among the first few black students at this recently integrated institution of higher learning. We learned quickly that if we wanted privacy, all the two of us had to do was sit down in the lobby of a campus building. We didn't have to worry about too many people sitting next to us – talk about social distancing, right? We would walk into the student center or university library and laugh afterward about how many stares we got before we could even find a seat. Some students even moved to another table if we sat too close to them, but most were cordial and seemed to be more concerned with their studies than with black students being on campus. There were a few white students who seemed to go out of their way to speak or shoot the breeze when they saw us, which was very reassuring most days.

It was nice having Robert and the other few blacks there with me. There was something about seeing someone who you could share that experience with, especially since there were no black faculty members. I always thought about how difficult it would be if I had been the only black student on campus, but the truth is, most of the time, it still felt like I was all alone anyway.

I continued to commute daily to SLU, succeeding in the classroom and helping to "break the color line" so to speak, at that historic institution. I also worked at the pool hall in Kinloch my entire four years in college, learning and sharpening my entrepreneurial skills as time went by.

I graduated with honors from SLU, and although it did not set in immediately, I realized more each day that I had done something special. Along with a handful of other black students, I had proven that blacks, regardless of their background, could compete and succeed in an academic environment, with white students, at a high level. I was there to get an education and move on to the next step in my life, but it turned out to be a more meaningful experience as was the case quite often for blacks who were first to accomplish something back in the day. My parents and family were proud of me, and it was extremely gratifying for me as well. Now I would get an opportunity to prove myself in the work world – Or would I?

I was enjoying all the congratulations and well-wishes from family, friends, neighbors, and some of my former teachers seemed as elated as me. All that attention made me feel like a real celebrity, although I didn't think much about my future for about a week or two. I chose to pursue the private sector for employment to explore my mathematical skills in the business world. If it did not work out, I could always become a teacher. I had followed my mother's and my older sister's advice to obtain teaching credentials before graduating from St. Louis University. My older sister, Pauline, and my mother advised me that the highest-level employment for black college graduates was in teaching, preaching, or working as a clerk for the post office.

Soon, I began my search for employment in the private sector, and my first target was McDonnell Aircraft Manufacturing. I sent my resume and was asked to appear for an interview. My resume indicated that I had a degree in Mathematics from St. Louis University. It did not dawn on me that I may have been the first black man with the audacity to apply for professional employment at McDonnell, and among the first blacks to graduate from a previously all-white college or university in a former slave state. On the day of that interview, I was as "clean as the board of health", dressed in a black suit and tie and filled with excitement and optimism in anticipation of what may be next for me. After all, in my mind, I deserved it after proving myself at SLU. When I arrived for the interview, I was greeted by a McDonnell employee, who asked, "May I help you?" I stated my name and said, "I am here for a ten o'clock job interview." Then the employee paused, glanced at the resume he was holding in his left hand, and with a patronizing look on his face, he responded, "I'm so sorry Mr. Clay, but someone obviously made a mistake because we do not have jobs here at McDonnell for professional Negros. I apologize for the misunderstanding and do have a safe trip home." Just like that, I was heading back out the door without an interview or even an insincere handshake. I was shocked and extremely disappointed with what had just occurred. I felt hurt and embarrassed. Should I have known?

Obviously, the McDonnell hiring office did not realize I was black because on paper I was an honors graduate in mathematics from St. Louis University, *so how could Roy Clay be a Negro?* They never expected a graduate with my credentials to be black. Some graduates from Lincoln University, a St. Louis area HBCU, must have applied there, but their applications were probably trashed or never responded to. I walked away with my head bowed but reflecting on my mother's guidance about not allowing racism or discrimination to be a reason for me not to succeed. I arrived home, and my parents could see how disappointed I was from the dejected look on my face. There was nothing they could do other than encourage me that a change would come someday.

In my mind, I was not going to give up seeking employment in the corporate world, but I needed a job, so I decided to stop by the post office and apply for a job as a clerk. My education alone more than qualified me for the job, as was the case for many other black college graduates who were being hired there. I went to my family doctor, Dr. Roy Johnson, to take the physical examination that was required.

After anxiously awaiting the medical exam results for a few days, I was notified that I did not pass the physical examination, as my body was not the same after the injury I suffered as a boy. How could that be since I was ordered to take a physical examination for induction into the U.S. Army a couple months later, and I passed the exam? I received orders to report to the Army, but when I questioned the Army regarding my ability to be fit for the military but not for a job as a postal clerk, they changed my status, and I was reclassified as 4F (unfit to serve in the military). Therefore, I did not enter the armed forces.

Fortunately, I had acquired teaching credentials at SLU, which made it possible for me to apply and be hired to teach in the still segregated St. Louis public schools. I taught for about one year, and it was extremely rewarding to help those young people in every way I could. They were just like me when I was their age: intelligent, bright-eyed, with unlimited potential, but with little support from their communities and in an unequal world. I was their teacher, but some days I had to be their counselor, coach, big brother, and even a father figure. I met some very dedicated educators while teaching, and I think I helped some kids along the way.

In 1952, I ended my teaching career. Teaching mathematics and English grammar was the most satisfying job I have ever held. However, at $232 per month, I could barely afford an automobile. The salaries they paid us at those segregated schools were merely a fraction of what they paid the white teachers at that time, and there was no sign of any change coming in the immediate future. That being so, I decided to move on and accept an offer of employment that paid more money from the US Small Arms Defense Corporation in St. Louis. The Korean War was still going on, and I was now a production line inspector and supervisor of the assembly of small arms ammunition that the armed forces would use in that war and other conflicts around the world. I am grateful for this job, not only for the extra money I was being paid but also because it enabled me to meet my wife of 38 years. She was truly an angel sent from heaven.

Shortly after entering the new job at U.S. Small Arms Defense Corporation, a new employee, Virginia Conners, was hired and assigned as a subordinate to me. She was so different from the others whose work I inspected, and she caught my attention more than any other woman I had ever known, including the girl I was dating at that time. I noticed how meticulous she was in performing her work, but that was not all I noticed. Her presence commanded attention whenever she entered a room, beginning with her walk, her style of dress, and then her quiet unassuming manner. I thought to myself, *now this is a real classy young lady.* I wanted to know more about her, what she liked and what her interests were. I had met a couple of women during my college days and there was a woman whom I was dating, someone I met while I was teaching school, but no one had ever caught my eye like Virginia. Somehow, I knew she was extra special from the moment we first met.

I kept the relationship professional for a while as I contemplated the best way to approach her. In time, I discovered that she occasionally enjoyed eating chocolate during her afternoon breaks. So, a few days later, I just happened to bring some chocolates to work, and I offered her some. She took the candy, thanked me, and smiled. This was the moment in which I had finally gathered enough courage to ask her for a date – Yes, this would be unacceptable in today's work environment, but it was not inappropriate in 1952. She hesitated initially, and then she told me I could meet her at the Barcelona, a local bar and restaurant, after work.

This was all happening faster than I expected, so there were no words for how excited I was to get to know her personally. I was so nervous that in my anxiety, I made a careless mistake while driving over to the Barcelona Lounge. I pulled up to a stop sign and looked in my rearview mirror for an instant. Then I pressed the accelerator before I turned back to the front, and I rear-ended the car in front of me that had not yet departed. The loud crashing sound of our fenders colliding at that intersection attracted the attention of many onlookers, but I was hoping Virginia was not in sight or sound of this embarrassing mess I had caused. The older man whose car I damaged was very demonstrative as he took my driver's license and contact information and yelled at me for being so careless. If Virginia had witnessed this accident, that would be the end of our relationship before it even started, I thought. The vehicle damage was not as bad as it could have been, I suppose, and I was a little late arriving to meet her, but once I settled down and we started talking, it was very apparent that this was the woman for me. I just prayed that she felt the same about me as I felt about her. She was very calm and understanding when I explained to her what happened, and at the end of the evening, she agreed to go out again, which was a good sign of things to come.

Things were going well with the job as I was developing more people skills and sharpening my leadership abilities in my role as an inspector/supervisor. I also found myself stocking up on chocolates and smiling a lot at Virginia. Whenever I flashed my unforgettable smile, she would giggle, sometimes wink, but she managed to stay focused on her work. She was unquestionably the best employee in the department. Moments like that had me feeling like a high school freshman experiencing his first crush. My first private date with Virginia was at a movie theater in University City, St. Louis County, which had just begun to admit black customers. Virginia lived with her mother, three older brothers, and two younger sisters. My family home in Kinloch was even more crowded. The significance of going on that date to watch a movie was that it provided the privacy we both sought. Also, we were both dating other partners whom our families expected us to marry at the time. However, after that date, we knew we were meant to be together. Frankly, I knew I wanted to marry her; it was just a matter of time. I know it may seem fast, but sometimes you just know. By the way, the theme song from that movie soundtrack was "Our Love Is Here to Stay." Naturally, that song became our favorite from that point in our relationship, and it still has a sentimental value to me when I hear it even now.

Virginia and I enjoyed learning about each other's family history and backgrounds as we spent more and more time together. Virginia talked about her dad passing when she was ten years old and how she had to grow up in a hurry to help her mom since she was the oldest daughter. She had three older brothers and two younger sisters. Her mother worked a lot, so Virginia was practically the head of the household by the time she was sixteen. So, when other girls started dating and socializing, she had to step in and help take care of her siblings. Additionally, she worked at a local retail store where she was known as the beautiful lady who sold peanuts and jellybeans. She remained on that job until she gained employment at the U.S. Small Arms Defense Corporation, where we met. The more familiar I became with her, the more I liked this woman who seemed so giving and unselfish.

Virginia graduated from Vashon High School in St. Louis, which was only five or six miles from my high school in Webster Groves, and a rival black school in the area. One autumn evening, after work, we were sharing a pop and taking in the colorful fall foliage at sunset at one of our favorite parks. She told me that she once went on a date sometime in 1946 with one of my high school classmates. It happened to be a guy who was our only four-letter athlete at

Douglas High. Naturally, I was feeling a little insecure at first, but then she said he mentioned to her that he had a classmate who was so smart that he had the highest IQ recorded in the history of our high school. She said that he referred to me by name, and she remembered thinking at that time how wonderful it would be to meet someone like that because she admired intelligent guys. I talked to her about my upbringing in Kinloch, and about my parents and siblings. She seemed to be amazed at my desire to be the best at everything that I did, and she was very attracted to my commitment to getting a good education. She said, "It's not every day you meet a young colored (black) man who is so well educated and knowledgeable." She went on to say that she valued that in a man. This was different for me since I had never heard that from the previous women I had dated.

You may believe that those strangely fortuitous occurrences that preceded Virginia and I coming together may have been a foreshadowing of things to come, but I say falling in true love and being compatible from the very beginning was a sign to me that *our love was here to stay*. And, oh by the way, after only a few months of our courtship, my parents and family seemed to enjoy Virginia's company almost as much as I did. It was the same for me regarding Virginia's family. They lived in the city of St. Louis, so it was a more fast-paced life, with paved roads and bright city lights, but there was a chemistry between us that black folks seemed to always share no matter where they were from. Her older brothers, Lou, Bob, and Charles (nicknamed June

Bug), along with sisters Violet (nicknamed Lucky) and Joyce, welcomed me warmly despite their fondness for Virginia's previous fiancé. They knew that he was upset when Virginia broke off their engagement, but they also realized that if their sister was breaking up with him to be with me, then I must have been a special guy.

They respected Virginia, or "Nooky" (pronounced Nukey) as they called her back then, and supported her decision to be with me. It didn't hurt that I always came to visit as they said, "in a nice, shiny car, and was very well dressed." That, along with being, in their words, "very smart" seemed to seal the deal, and the family immediately liked me. Mrs. Conners, Virginia's mother, thought the world of her, so she was pleased with the decision and was very cordial with me whenever we saw each other, which was not often because she worked long and difficult hours. Virginia was the spitting image of her mother, who, after being widowed at a relatively young age with six children to raise, was a serious, quiet woman most of the time. It was almost as if it was her way of holding back tears from the unfortunate hand she had been dealt in life. Understandably, she did not smile often, but she always had a smile and a hug for me. She said she admired me for being so well educated, which apparently meant a lot to her. I did not get to know Virginia's older brother Lou very well because he had started working early to help feed the family after the sudden death of their dad. By this time, he was a grown man living on his own.

As the oldest daughter in the house, Virginia was like a mother to the younger sisters, "Lucky" and Joyce. She was especially motherly towards Joyce, who is ten years younger than her. She bought clothes for Joyce, combed her hair, and helped her with schoolwork. Their mother was not very stern and had designated Virginia the leader of the girls, which caused "Lucky" and Virginia to butt heads since they were closer in age. Joyce got her disciplining from Virginia if she did not follow the rules of the house, but she was ten years younger, so she seemed to have no problem with Virginia being the leader of the household when their mother was not around. All the while, I was observing Virginia and thinking how wonderful she would be as a mother.

Virginia and I were doing well on our respective jobs. Still, I was continually applying for jobs in mathematics throughout the St. Louis area. I was determined to get a job in my field, and Virginia always reminded me to keep trying, and something good would eventually happen. The two of us discussed the plight of blacks in America many times, hoping things would get better someday. We even discussed me going back into the education field when the landmark Supreme Court Case "Brown vs. Board of Education" ruled that the segregation of children because of race in public schools was unconstitutional in 1954. One year later, the Supreme Court directed the school boards to proceed with desegregation with all deliberate speed, so still, nothing had changed, and some local officials even defied it. I thought to myself, *there is no way I will go back into teaching – there must be something in mathematics in my future.* It's just a matter of time. I knew I wanted to marry Virginia, so it would be important to start a career in my field.

I was still learning so much about this woman I was committed to and enjoying every moment of it. I learned that she had been very smart as a high school student and was an honor society member. Her younger sister Joyce mentioned recently how she still recalls going to Virginia's graduation ceremony at Vashon High School and seeing her being honored that day. Unfortunately, Virginia's mother couldn't afford to send her to college, so she had to start working at that five-and-dime store after high school. She attended Stowe Junior College part-time after saving a little money from her paycheck at the store. Joyce used to visit Virginia while she was working at the five-and-dime store, and she says Virginia would always give her peanuts and jellybeans. That always made Joyce's day and was a big thrill for her because she often brought her closest friends along with her. They couldn't enter the store, but they would wait outside for Joyce and her big sister Virginia so they could all partake of the peanuts and sweets.

Four years after Virginia and I met, two life-changing events took place for both of us. To the surprise of no one, Virginia and I were married in St. Louis on June 30, 1956. Although we did not spend much money on the wedding, it was memorable and a wonderful day for our families. The song that had become our theme song, "Our Love Is Here to Stay," was played that day, and I whispered each word of the lyrics softly in her ear as we danced at a small reception afterward. She could not have been more beautiful that day, and together, we could not have been happier. Shortly after, I was hired by McDonnell Aircraft in 1956, near Ferguson. Yes, the same McDonnell that would not even interview me in 1952 because of the color of my skin. I just kept applying, and by and by, they either changed their way of thinking, or they just got tired of looking at my applications – probably a little of both. Still, I never gave up, and it paid off.

I suppose times were also changing in the world of technology. At McDonnell Aircraft, I had an opportunity to learn about computers. Contemporary technology moguls, Bill Gates and Steve Jobs, were still in diapers back then. If they only knew what wondrous things were in their future. As a matter of fact, my colleagues and I were among the leaders in the field, and we didn't know it. At the time, there was no discipline known as Computer Science. Intel Corporation did not exist. Microsoft, Google, Apple, Yahoo, Facebook, and others came decades later. Still, there I was, a mathematician working in computer programming, not realizing I was on the front side of "the digital divide" and just steps away from my journey through Silicon Valley.

Chapter Four

CALIFORNIA HERE WE COME

St. Louis had experienced a great deal of growth until the 1950s. It had been one of America's largest cities. The downtown area looked different without today's skyscrapers and the now-familiar Arch that was not completed until 1965. However, it still had a big city kind of feel compared to some other Midwest towns. Sitting on the west bank of the massive Mississippi River, St. Louis was connected to East St. Louis, Illinois, by the Eads Bridge, which had spanned above the mighty river since 1874. It was the world's first all-steel bridge at the time of completion. Up until the early 50s, the bright lights of Grand Boulevard were shining their brightest, and the Union Station area, near Eads Bridge, was a bustling transportation hub. Primary industries included aviation, transportation, and the food and beverage manufacturing industry, most notably the Anheuser-Busch Brewery. There were unskilled labor jobs and steady paying skilled work as well. The city's pastimes were baseball, beer, jazz, blues, and its vibrant nightlife. That city life made "The

Gateway to the West" a better place for the blacks who had moved from the slow-paced rural life and fields of Alabama, Arkansas, Louisiana, and Mississippi.

The churches in St. Louis were a little larger, some with slightly taller steeples, and more immaculate than those in the South, or those I had seen over in Kinloch. They were often led by dapper-dressed, fast-talking preachers who sermonized messages of hope to their God-loving faithful. Churches were places where folks gathered socially to make lasting friendships and sometimes meet their future spouses. It was a decent place to live. However, with the crowded conditions and lack of jobs in the many neighborhoods, the crime rate was a bit high. Unfortunately, that was typical of most large cities, even in those days. The city was about twice the size in population as it is today.

Virginia and I lived with my Uncle Walter when we were first married. He was my mother's brother and had a small home in the Compton Hills section of St. Louis. We didn't know it then, but famed author and poet, Maya Angelou's birthplace was in that same neighborhood. Virginia thought it would be a good idea for her baby sister, Joyce, to move in with us, and I agreed since Virginia had practically raised her. She lived with us from the very beginning. Luckily, we found an apartment a few months later in the same general neighborhood, east of Grand Avenue in Midtown. It was a blessing to be able to move into our own place.

I remember being advised about where to live in St. Louis by my Uncle Walter at a Saturday afternoon Cardinals baseball game at Sportsmen's Park. We both loved the game, and since there had been no Negro League baseball in St. Louis since Satchell Paige and his Kansas City Monarchs came to town for an exhibition game in 1941, we were Cardinals fans by default. You see, the Cardinals and the St. Louis Browns of the American League (now the Baltimore Orioles) were the last Major League Baseball teams with seating restrictions for black fans, so it took a while for blacks to warm up to baseball at Sportsmen's Park, now known as Busch Stadium. He told me that he was at that last Negro League game and that the racist restrictions were lifted for that one game because Paige had refused to play if they didn't change the rule for that gameday. There was a record crowd that day, and it was the game when Paige waved in his outfielders one inning and struck out the batter with his "trouble ball" to the fans' delight. He said nobody in the world could hit that pitch. The seating restrictions were finally lifted in the mid-1940s, a few years after that daring Satchell Paige demonstration. We had good seats that day, in early 1957, as we watched the Cardinals play the Cubs.

Between innings, I mentioned to my uncle that I was going to stay in the city and that I was looking for an apartment. Then he leaned over to me and whispered, "If you are going to stay in St. Louis, just remember that there are certain parts of the city where you are not wanted and having that St. Louis University degree doesn't matter." I took that not only as advice but as a wake-up call. That advice reminded me that a degree didn't change the color of my skin and that my race still mattered. At that moment, with two outs and the bases loaded, it did not matter who was coming up to bat. That's when I knew that I wanted to help make things better. I wanted to help make a difference – like Satchell Paige.

We didn't have many options of where to live in St. Louis, which was typical of many American cities at the time. The Pruitt-Igoe apartment complex was on the North Side, not far from the river, but was a low-income housing project, supposedly for the working class. You know what that meant: working-class "Negroes" as we were labeled. With over 30 new buildings, rising 11 stories each, it quickly became the largest and most symbolic of the social, racial, and community tensions that plagued America's cities during that era. It opened between 1954 and 1956, but the project eventually became a disaster for all the usual reasons that occur when you crowd too many poor people into a small area. Just as in other major cities across the country, white residents were leaving for the suburbs as "white flight" was taking place because the Brown vs. Board of Education verdict in 1954 opened the door for broad desegregation in St. Louis. During the brief years that Pruitt-Igoe existed, the buildings were always in disrepair because of cheap building materials and a poor maintenance record, which added to the deterioration of the complex. The entire compound was demolished in the early 1970s.

Just across the river, the East St. Louis massacre of 1917 was indicative of racial tension in the country also, as blacks were demanding equal rights and job opportunities. A series of labor and race-related incidents of violence by white residents resulted in as many as 250 blacks being killed in the Summer of 1917. Another 6,000 black residents were left homeless due to burning and vandalism. All of this was caused by the hiring of black employees at a previously all-white war industry factory just outside of East St. Louis, Illinois. Many displaced blacks sought refuge across the river in St. Louis, where housing and employment were already scarce.

Like many other urban areas, there was not much housing for middle-income earners of color like me. I wanted to live in 'The Ville' area of the city, but McDonnell was not paying me well, so the rental properties there were not affordable for me. It was a nicer, more established black neighborhood for the most part. It was also where the historic Sumner High School, the first high school for blacks West of the Mississippi River, was located. Sumner was a rival to the other black high schools in the St. Louis area, including Kinloch High School, Vashon, Virginia's school, and my high school, Frederick Douglass, in Webster Groves. Sumner was the oldest school, and the list of distinguished alumni from Sumner reads like a Who's Who. Notables like Arthur Ashe, Tina Turner, Chuck Berry, Grace Bumbry, Ethel Hedgeman Lyle (Founder of Alpha Kappa Alpha Sorority), my college friend, Robert Guillaume, and many more graduated from there.

I was enjoying my family, the apartment, and working probably twice as hard as the other guys at the office. It paid off, too, as the experience and knowledge I gained working at McDonnell proved to be the turning point of my career. I always thought that I would major in mathematics, get a degree, and become a mathematician if I could get hired – as jobs just were not a sure thing for a black man in the 1950s. I was always an observant guy, which led me to realize that the business world was changing. Just a few years earlier, businesses were not using computers much at all. This was the first period of computer technology; some of them weighed over 30 tons, took up a lot of space, and required a large room to house these new monstrous creations. Besides the fact that not many folks knew much about them, it was my opinion that technological innovations would follow to make computers more compatible with the work environment. That occurred with the second generation of computers which ran from about 1956 to 1963. The new machines utilized transistors instead of the big, cumbersome vacuum tubes that were previously used, thus allowing computers to be smaller in size, faster in speed, and less expensive to build. I was fortunate, as mathematicians were often considered best suited to assist in the operation and programming of this new technology. You see, computer science or computer technology programs in higher education were rare at the time. Finally, it did not matter what color you were - white, black, red, blue, or purple; if you had the ability to code and program, you were the right man, or woman, for the job. I was in the right place at the right time, it seemed, and as always, I was up for the challenge and excited about my future in technology.

There were only a handful of black professionals working at the McDonnell facility when I was hired. I brought a little color to the weekly staff meetings. I couldn't help but remember when I was told that they did not hire "Negros" when I applied for a job there in the past, but this was a new day, thanks to the new computer age, and I was determined to learn whatever I needed to know to become an expert in the field of computer programming. I worked late hours almost every workday learning as much as I could and practicing my program writing skills. It was sort of a love affair between me and that big computer on those lonely nights. Sure, there were many holdovers there who did not consider me as their equal in the beginning. It is also quite possible that I may have been just a token hire, but I think they really needed me – just not as a manager, though. However, it was a great chance for me to learn about programming, even if I had to teach myself. Times seemed to be changing, and I wanted to stay on top of my game. So, when the right opportunity came along, I wanted to be ready.

It was always uplifting to spend my evenings relaxing with my new wife, Virginia, who often reassured me that I must continue to work harder than anyone else and remember that giving respect every day would be the best way to earn respect and succeed in that environment. She also helped me to understand early in our marriage that the concepts of love and respect were synonymous. She had become as significant as my mother at this point in my life by encouraging me to follow the words that I always tried to live by, such as - "Do the best you know how at any pursuit, and don't brag, don't complain and don't explain. Just perform as best you know how." That was Virginia – always helping me to stay the course. She did not finish college herself because of a strong dedication to help her mother with the other children, especially her younger sisters, so she had only taken a few classes at Stowe Jr College. However, she was a firm believer in pursuing higher education and setting career goals.

We did not waste much time starting our family, as was typical of most couples back in the day. Birth control, what was that? Our first child, Roy, Jr, was born in November 1957. I was a proud father, and that was something I had always dreamed of, but it happened a lot sooner than I thought it would. I had a son to carry my name on already, who was keeping us up at night and giving us another human being to put before ourselves. Now there were four of us, including Joyce. It warmed my heart as I watched Virginia care for Roy, Jr. I knew early on that I had chosen the right woman to be the mother of my children.

During this time, I met Clifton Gates, a successful black professional in St. Louis. He and I became best friends within a few months. We leaned on each other for wisdom since there were not many black men who were fortunate enough to be in the positions we were in. In 1958, Clifton visited the San Francisco Bay Area with his wife. When he returned, we all got together to hear about this trip to the West Coast. He was not normally a very emotional or expressive kind of guy, but I will never forget the look of joy and wonderment in his eyes as he described the Bay Area, the Pacific Ocean, the Golden Gate Bridge, and the overall beauty he had experienced. He also said that the people out West were more laid back and seemed more hospitable. I was sold on California right away, and after a few weeks, both Clifton and I promised to someday move to San Francisco, California as our careers would probably never break through the proverbial "glass ceiling" at our jobs in the St. Louis area.

I immediately started to apply for positions in the Bay Area, and soon I was invited to an interview in St. Louis for a computer programming position at the Lawrence Radiation Laboratory in Livermore, California. I wanted this position, and Virginia was all for moving West as well. I had two days to prepare for the interview and prayed I would impress the hiring officials. Well, I aced the interview and was offered the position right away. I did not hesitate to accept the offer since I already had Virginia's approval. Maya Angelou, who was born in Missouri a year before me, once said, "If you are going down a road and don't like what's in front of you and look behind you and don't like what you see, get off the road. Create a new path!" Virginia and I believed in those words, so there was no hesitation in deciding to get on this new road. Virginia always seemed to keep me on the right path. I gave McDonnell notice that I would be leaving, and just like that, my life and future drastically changed. It wasn't a sure thing; nothing ever is, but in our hearts, we knew it was the best thing. We had to pack up what little we had and prepare for this trip, but we were moving to the West Coast, and the potential to fulfill our dreams was endless and exciting.

The American Dream was more evident in the 1950s than in any other decade before it. There were more jobs. It was the baby boom era, and families were buying homes and cars at an all-time high. This was not usually the case for Black Americans, however. This was especially true of places like Missouri, but just maybe we could make that happen in California, a place for new beginnings, where rapid growth was happening at the time. Why, even my favorite baseball team, the Brooklyn Dodgers, moved to Los Angeles that same year, minus the retired legend Jackie Robinson, of course. The New York Giants and superstar Willie Mays also decided to go West, choosing San Francisco as their new home. I kept thinking that I just may get a glimpse of Mays passing me on Route 66 West, and that would be worth the trip by itself.

I had so much planning to do before I embarked on this journey. I also wanted to say goodbye to friends and family. That would be difficult because I had no idea when I would be returning to Missouri. The most difficult moment came on my last visit to Kinloch. I will never forget my going away celebration that was held at my parent's house. Most of my family was there to wish me well and tell me how proud they were of me. My mother said a prayer and served some of the best fried chicken and corn on the cob west of the Mississippi. My father and big brother, Charles, just looked at me and hugged me more times than I could count fingers on my hands.

I also stopped by the Pool Hall to bid my farewell to the people I had worked for. That place helped me get through college. Some folks there asked if I was afraid, and I responded, "Everything we do carries some level of risk, but that should not stop you from living your life." I went on to say, "If I don't take this opportunity, I may never get the chance again." It was my opinion even then that, no risk equals no rewards. Everyone wished me well, and they all said they wished they had the guts to make the move I was making. You see, most folks felt comfortable with the life they had in Kinloch, but not me. My intuition was telling me, "Go West, young man" and that's exactly where I was headed. I couldn't wait to smell the saltwater mist in the air and feel a big fat wave against my face when I reached the Pacific Ocean.

There was so much happening in 1958. U.S. President Dwight D. Eisenhower signed the National Aeronautics and Space Act into law, creating the National Aeronautics and Space Administration, more commonly referred to as NASA. America launched its first satellite, the Explorer 1, from Cape Canaveral, an important milestone in the earliest years of the space race between the United States and the Soviet Union

(USSR). Several other U.S. satellites followed. The Sputnik satellite had been launched by the USSR the previous year, and they had launched a couple more as well. Nikita Khrushchev was now the Premier of the Soviet Union. Also, St. Louis native, W.C. Handy, who composed "St. Louis Blues", and who many consider the father of Blues, passed away in New York City.

The Microchip was co-invented by Jack Kilby of Texas Instruments and Robert Noyce of Fairchild in 1958. Semiconductors were later developed and marketed in the U.S. by Intel. The integrated circuit, an essential piece of technology used in modern electronics, was created by Kilby, a newly hired engineer at Texas Instruments, who came up with the idea to miniaturize the parts of a whole transistor circuit and join them together, creating a smaller and much easier to use produce unit called an integrated circuit. There were other persons credited with the idea of an integrated circuit. Still, Kilby was the first to produce a working model and file a patent for the technology. The creation of this integrated circuit would certainly set the stage for some of my future professional accomplishments, as it has since truly led to much of the technology our modern computers and electronics are based on today. And to think, it was the same year I moved to the Bay Area, the place where my career would take off.

We had to plan our trip very carefully because there were few places between St Louis and San Francisco where black travelers could stop for food, overnight accommodations, or even restrooms, and we were traveling with a child who was less than a year old. It was time to pull out the "Green Book," which was a source that provided information on hotels, restaurants, gas stations, and other businesses that would accommodate blacks while traveling across the country. Charles had a copy of it and gave it to me as a going-away gift. He said I would need it a lot more now than he would. He was married now, living in Detroit, and came down to visit me when my parents had the going away party.

I was going to miss St. Louis, Kinloch, SLU, the never-ending southward flow of the Mississippi River, and even the McDonnell workplace and a few of my colleagues whom I had worked so closely with. However, there was so much promise ahead, and it was time to hit the road. Gasoline was only 25 cents a gallon, so I filled up the tank with just a little more than 3 dollars. Things sure have changed, right? I made sure the car was serviced a week earlier, so we were ready to travel. I was the driver starting out, with Virginia next to me in the front and Joyce taking care of Roy, Jr in the back seat.

I had mapped it out to 2300 miles total, from St. Louis to Los Angeles and ending in San Francisco. The first stop in L.A. would be to stay with my sister, Imogene, the first in the family to make the trip West. She married a Missouri guy at a young age, with a little one on the way. A few years later, they moved to South Central, L.A, which had become a popular area for Black Californians at the time. We planned to stay with her for a couple of weeks and then continue to our ultimate destination, the San Francisco Bay Area, where we were to stay with my cousin Delores temporarily until we found a permanent home.

Neither of us had ever driven more than the 300 miles, from St. Louis to Chicago, which was only one time before this trip. We were told it would take about 4 days with stops, so we were prepared for that. Virginia's mother and my parents asked us to check in by phone every other day to let them know how we were doing on our journey. I knew they would be worried until we arrived in California and would want to hear from us. There were no cell phones or laptops back in the day, so the plan was to call collect from motel rooms or a public phone booth. GPS did not exist; however, we had excellent road maps, some good old common sense, and my mother's prayers. That's all we needed - so I thought.

The historic Route 66, or "The Mother Road," as some called it, ran from Chicago to Los Angeles. We got on in downtown St. Louis near the Mississippi River and headed West, to the Kansas state line, 300 miles away and just west of Joplin, Missouri. I had never driven to that side of the state, so I was curious to see how different it would be. Also, I had heard Joplin mentioned on Nat King Cole's 1946 recording, 'Route 66,' which was a song Virginia and I had danced to often. Driving through Missouri was rather charming as we cruised along in my 1956 Black Ford with white interior, but unfortunately, no air conditioning. It was a fine-looking automobile, though. As you can imagine, the large trunk compartment was loaded with our belongings, but there were a few things we would have shipped to us once we settled into the Bay Area. We were in Springfield before we knew it, and then it was on to Joplin after passing through some smaller towns.

Before we reached Joplin, we had to make a gasoline stop at the service station that sat on a corner, adjacent to a country store with a full porch and a confederate flag perched from the railing. There were railroad tracks behind the store, running parallel to the highway. We were in Carthage, Missouri, and it is where Virginia would take the wheel to give me a short break. Besides the flag next door, it was very peaceful looking, but sometimes that can be misleading. I did not see one black person, although there was a "colored" restroom, so it did not take me long to figure out that there were black folks around somewhere. The young, bearded attendant who greeted us was courteous, and he especially did not hesitate to point us in the direction of the "colored" rest room. We did not encounter any problems while there, and we did not have to refer to the Green Book. We just got a few curious looks from folks, but that was expected, especially when they saw who was driving that shiny late-model automobile. Joyce changed little Roy's diaper after he had been sleeping most of the morning, and soon we were back on the road.

As we approached Joplin, I could not help but wonder if it was named for the ragtime composer Scott Joplin, who lived in Sedalia, Missouri. Then I saw a billboard that read,

"Welcome to Joplin. Home of Reverend Harris Joplin, an early settler and the founder of the area's first Methodist congregation." That sign was old and weathered, and I joked with Virginia, saying, "It appeared old enough that Reverend Joplin could have posted it himself." The next billboard advertised the city's most famous saloon, which once boasted a bar and restaurant on the first floor, gambling on the second, and a brothel on the third back in the old days. It seems that trolley and rail lines had made Joplin the hub of Southwest Missouri. I wondered what Reverend Joplin thought about that wild history. The city was known for its mining and the notorious Bonnie and Clyde, who hid there in 1933. Despite being one of the more medium-sized cities in Missouri, there was a quietness and attractively old-fashioned feel as we continued carefully through the city, but I had no intention of stopping.

We enjoyed the picturesque rural views along the highway as we snacked on some food we had brought along. Virginia had made some of her special chicken sandwiches, packed a few apples, and a small cooler filled with bottles of pop, so we had enough food and drinks to last for the day. I couldn't help but notice that there were very few people who looked like us in Joplin. So naturally, we slowed down and minded the speed limit, as my father had reminded us to do before we left, and now it was California or bust. Our next stop was in Kansas. Now, what could we expect there?

Before long, we were crossing into Kansas. I had heard about it from watching a few Western movies, but I would not learn much about it on this trip as Kansas was the shortest of all the states we traveled through. Only 13 miles as we quickly passed by Galena and a few other places I can't remember. It felt good to get through another state, though, and I recall announcing to the family, "We're in Oklahoma now; that's progress." I got some applause from Joyce, a smile from Virginia, and Roy, Jr just kept on sleeping. Commerce, Oklahoma, is where I took over driving again. We were less than two short hours away from Tulsa, Oklahoma, where we had plenty of suggestions from the Green Book regarding where to stop for the night.

I was so happy to arrive in Tulsa after a long day's ride. The stretch of Route 66 from St. Louis to Tulsa was considered the heart of Route 66. It's where the Midwest links up with the West, so reaching Tulsa was like a milestone moment. We were looking forward to seeing this city, even though it was known for the Greenwood race massacre that occurred in 1921. Many restaurants and motels were listed in Tulsa by Green Book as businesses that welcomed "The Negro Traveler," and we were ready to relax before getting back on the road the following day. We had to get off the main highway for a few miles and go into the city to get to the hotel and restaurant we had chosen from the Green Book. We wanted to try the Del Rio Hotel on Greenwood Avenue, not far from the original Greenwood District and on the other side of the tracks. There appeared to be some revitalization in that surrounding area, including this old three-story brick building with a charming double door entrance that was the

Del Rio. We parked in the rear, checked in, and realized it was black-owned as we were greeted with warm smiles and treated like family during that one-night stay. I went out to pick up some chili dogs, coleslaw, and fries at Art's Chili Parlor. I spoke to Art, a tall, dark, middle-aged Tulsan, who thanked me for stopping by and wished me well on my move to the West Coast, and whispered to me, "Ask the folks at Del Rio to tell you about the Greenwood Race Riot." I told him, "I plan to." I then went back to the hotel; we enjoyed our meal and called it an early night. And oh, by the way, those chili dogs were "mighty good" as advertised.

In the morning, we would learn about that deadly massacre by whites in the black area called Black Wall Street. It was where black workers spent their earnings in a bustling, booming city within Tulsa. We sat back on a couch in the motel's tiny lobby area as we listened to a staffer explain that there were once blocks of Black-owned businesses before the riot. "You name it, Greenwood had it," he boasted. The Greenwood district also had 15 doctors, a hospital, two dentists, three lawyers, a library, two schools, and two black newspaper publishers and bankers. We were told that it all started because of a sensationalized story of a black male teenager having inappropriate behavior with a seventeen-year-old white girl in an elevator. When a white mob tried to lynch the black teenager, a group of black citizens tried to rescue him, but they were easily outnumbered and overwhelmed. The mob commenced to leveling more than 35 city blocks. An estimated 191 businesses were destroyed, and roughly 10,000 Black residents were displaced from the neighborhood where they had lived, learned, played, worked, and prospered. Although the state declared the massacre death toll to be only 36 people, other estimates were as high as 300 deaths. As we listened to the people telling the story, it brought tears to our eyes. However, it was good to hear the truth and see the evidence of the massacre.

Virginia and I thanked the wonderful people who shared their story with us, we said a prayer together, and then we started back on our journey to the West Coast. This stop in Tulsa touched my soul in a way I had not felt before, but it enriched us with a sense of pride and reminded us of all we have overcome as strong, resilient Black Americans in our quest for freedom and equal rights. We drove by Vernon AME Church, where people hid in the basement for safety after the main floors of the building were blown away and burned. As I viewed the site, I thought that the spirit of those people and the souls, taken from us during that massacre, were still here with us, and my hope of things to come in California was invigorated while in Tulsa that day. Thus, it was more meaningful now to hit the road – Route 66 was looking better than ever.

According to the Route 66 song lyrics, "Oklahoma City is mighty pretty", and we were heading that way. I was at the wheel, and Joyce was in the front with me, while Virginia was in the back seat with little Roy. This would be our longest leg of the trip as our next stop was Albuquerque, New Mexico. It would be hard on Virginia and me, but we were feeling inspired after hearing the stories of our people's strength and resiliency in Tulsa. We stopped in Oklahoma City to fuel up and stretch our legs and see about the baby's needs, then we were headed for that long, flat Texas Panhandle on our way to another state, New Mexico. We ran into rain briefly as we approached Oklahoma City, but that was the only bad weather during the entire trip. After we stopped there at the service station, Virginia took over the driving. She drove for several hours as we crossed into the Texas Panhandle. This Northwest Corner of the State was flat and dry and sometimes had steady winds that would create mild dust storms in those days. We were aware of that and hoped we did not see that type of weather because we had to keep the windows down as we had no air conditioning in the car.

We arrived in Amarillo and stopped there mainly to pick up some sandwiches and let me handle the driving for the remainder of the day. This place had that old west kind of look and feel to it, with western wear shops and antique stores everywhere. That's something I had never seen before. Still, I was rudely reminded of how different it was for a black man traveling in America, the country my ancestors helped build. Across the road from the service station, there was a small diner, so I went inside to order some burgers for my family. Joyce accompanied me so that she could help me carry food back to the car. As I stood there, just inside the door, I noticed a small informal dining area with a few customers sitting at tables. The server eventually took the order and said with a not-so-friendly look, "You're going to eat this outside, right?" I felt so insulted with my young sister-in-law standing there beside me, who always looked up to me, and was now doing so literally. I took a deep breath and thought to myself, *yes, I intended to take my order to the car, but I wanted that to be my choice.* I swallowed my pride and paid him anyway.

When I got to the car, I reluctantly told my wife what had just happened, and I apologized to Joyce for not speaking up to that man. My wife told me that I did the right thing and advised me to put that incident behind me because we were safe, which was important to her and the family. She said, "Get back at that man by getting to California so that you can make a name for yourself." That sounded so much like my mother's response when I had the altercation with the Ferguson police as a teenager. This was another example of Virginia being that angel in my life when my mother was not around. I accepted being disrespected this time, but for good reason - to finish this trip and complete a goal. Still, I vowed to learn how to handle situations like this better in the future. Will Rogers said he never met a man he didn't like. After that day, I can't say the same, but my angels were guiding me in the right direction, to the West Coast on Route 66.

We were back on the road, heading towards New Mexico. After they consumed those sandwiches, I was the only one still awake in the car. It was just me, my road map, and miles of flat, desolate plains. The sun was directly in front of me, now, as the evening approached. So, the quote,

"Keep your face always toward the sunshine - and shadows will fall behind you," by Walt Whitman, couldn't be more applicable in this moment. I was leaving behind the negative thoughts from our last stop and pushing forward in positivity.

New Mexico not only looked different but had a different feel. I knew we had passed the halfway point in our trip, and that felt good. It was a more difficult drive because New Mexico's elevation along this path went from a high plateau area when we left Texas to the Sandia Mountains east of Albuquerque to over 7,200 feet at the Continental Divide near Thoreau. That made for a road surface with frequent twists, climbs, and descents. The family and I had no problem staying awake as we came closer to Albuquerque for a night's layover. The beautiful views of the high desert landscape were both austere and sublime, with its red-hued cliffs and valleys below. Motels and diners were plentiful along certain portions of Route 66, although they were probably not open to us. We crossed a bridge over the Rio Grande River and took out the map and the Green Book to find the motel we were hoping to stay at in Albuquerque. With only two places listed, we, fortunately, found Duncan's motel open to us on Arno Avenue rather easily, and after an extremely long and tiring day, I was ready to turn in, but first, we called our families from the modestly appointed double room. Then we took some time to get a quick bite to eat at a restaurant down the street called Aunt Brenda's. The food was superb – we all ordered the meatloaf, and her homemade iced tea hit the spot too. More importantly, it was nice to be able to sit down at a table together, to eat a meal, and use a restroom that was not labeled "Colored."

We slept well that night and got back on the road again after filling the car up with gas. We picked up some biscuits and fruit at Aunt Brenda's as well. It was another hot day, but we were not far away now. I could feel it. Like the Robert Frost passage, "Freedom is when you are easy in the harness," and that's the way I was feeling with the windows down and a smooth ride ahead. California was not far away. Before long, we crossed the Continental Divide and marveled at the incredible views. I supposed we were technically on the West Coast, so I told Virginia and Joyce. We all applauded, as we were another step closer to our destination. Roy Jr slept through the moment.

We crossed into Arizona, and the sweltering heat welcomed us. The beautiful and painted landscape, including rock formations and mesas, made for a picturesque and interesting drive, which helped keep our minds off the desert heat. We decided to stop, one more time, about 3 hours from L.A. The Green Book recommended White Rock Motel. It was located on the east end of Kingman, Arizona, directly on Route 66. We stayed there our last night, and again Green Book was right. They had a small café with excellent sandwiches and burgers, and the sunset seemed more spectacular in the West, like a canvas of warm colors.

The next morning, we made our stretch run to L.A. We stayed on Route 66 from the Arizona border, across San Bernardino County, into Pasadena, and South into Los Angeles. At one point, as we passed by a train on some tracks parallel to the highway, we started singing the Nat King Cole version of 'Route Sixty-Six' - *"When you make that California trip, Get your kicks on route sixty-six. Get your kicks on route sixty-six."* We must have sung those words for five or six minutes before reaching the "Los Angeles City Limit" sign. Even little Roy Jr smiled along with us. We used a map to guide us to my sister's address sometime around noon. It was a joy to arrive in South Central, L.A., and to hug my sister Imogene and her son Eathel. It was just as delightful to see her hold Roy Jr for the first time. We phoned our folks back home, and they were happy for us and relieved that we were safe. We made it across all those long, lonely roads, and now we were resting comfortably and feeling grateful. Los Angeles was unlike Kinloch or St. Louis. As much as I loved my home state of Missouri, I immediately noticed that California was different. The trees, flowers, homes, clothing styles, and the weather were all distinct. One thing I knew for sure – I would have to get used to it for better or worse because we were not in Missouri anymore.

Chapter Five

OPEN UP THAT GOLDEN GATE

After a good night's sleep in Los Angeles, my wife and I reflected on how blessed we were to have traveled over two thousand miles, through so many states, to arrive in California safely. That was something we did not take for granted. We were thankful for having a dependable automobile and grateful there was food, gasoline, and restrooms available along the way. Most of all, we were thankful for the motels that accommodated us so that we had somewhere safe to rest at night. That was typical of what most blacks prayed for when traveling America's highways during those years, and we were no different. That was the reality we lived with and why our mothers could not sleep until they received a call saying we had arrived at our destination safely. I saw unforgettable painted vistas and colorful sunsets on that drive out west. Still, the most memorable thing I experienced was meeting those descendants of the Tulsa massacre victims and standing on that sacred ground. I had tremendous admiration for those early business pioneers and sadness for how they lost their businesses. I felt something so deep in my soul that day that I will always take with me, and I vowed to myself to pass on the true history of what happened in Tulsa, as it was told to me.

Over the next couple of weeks, we got to know Los Angeles. The people, cultures, and cuisines were as fascinating as the near-perfect weather and the many beautiful beaches. Imogene was the perfect tour guide as we visited Hollywood, Beverly Hills, and other exciting attractions. When we returned to her modest, one-story home each evening, we would relax on the front porch, meet a few more of her neighbors, and plan for another day of adventure in the city of angels. The most exciting day was when we went to the beach for the first time, ever, in our lives. Joyce said, "I thought staying in a motel for the first time was great a few days ago, but this beach is something I never imagined." Virginia seemed to be speechless as she viewed the ocean for the first time, and for me, it was a thing of wonder. "Wow, the Pacific Ocean" were the first words I shouted. The seemingly never-ending sea, thunderous waves, scent of the saltwater mist softly blowing against my face, and miles of sandy beach were more than any picture or words could ever explain.

I was an adventurous kind of guy, so seeing our country from the great Mississippi all the way to the Pacific Ocean was something I always hoped for when I was growing up. Now, I was no Huck Finn, the Mark Twain character who was also from Missouri, along the Mississippi River, but going places and leaving my footprint on this earth was a dream of mine, just like it was for Huck. However, that and having a good heart was all I had in common with the Twain character. I was never afraid of adventure, and simply feeling that West Coast sand between my toes for the first time had me one step closer to my goals. Still, there would be other more challenging steps ahead in my journey to make some groundbreaking contributions in the field of technology.

Spending those three weeks in Los Angeles with my sister helped me feel more at home in California. I did not want to wear out my welcome, though, and my new employer was waiting on me; it was time to move on to San Francisco. We said our goodbyes to Imogene, dusted off our California map, and headed for the San Francisco Bay. It would be a ten-hour drive north, with plenty of picturesque coastal views and a promising future ahead. I promised Imogene we would return to see her, and we did many times, but now we were on our way to the Golden Gate.

The scenic and enjoyable drive up the Pacific Coast Highway had me wondering what took me so long to move out west. I was building a relationship with the West Coast. This place and I were compatible. The L.A. to San Francisco drive is well known as one of the world's prettiest and most scenic routes. We stopped in the beautiful city of San Luis Obispo, maybe because it sounded like St. Louis, but mostly because we were hungry. Imogene mentioned that there were some great places to grab lunch there, and boy was she right. There was a service station there also, so we were able to fill the car up. We passed through many picturesque cities, then Big Sur with its enormous waves crashing against the rugged garnet-hued rocks. There were countless other charming towns and memorable sights along the way. Then there was the San Francisco Bay and the wondrous Golden Gate Bridge. We didn't realize it then, but within one month, we had traveled on the two most storied and magnificent highways in America - Route 66 and the Pacific Coast Highway.

After arriving in the Bay Area, we stayed with Virginia's cousin, Delores, until we found a place of our own. We did some sightseeing the first few days in the Bay Area and learned so much about this part of California – the place I would call home for the remainder of my life. I was captivated by the history, alone, of this important cultural and business center of the west and storied entrance to the continent where the Pacific Ocean meets the San Francisco Bay. A tour guide mentioned that San Francisco became a city overnight after the discovery of gold in 1848, with thousands of people of every race and color hurrying to the "Golden Gate" in pursuit of wealth. Many of them made huge fortunes. The city also attracted black Americans from all over the country to what had become a boomtown because of high wages and opportunities during World War II. By the time we arrived, most of those jobs were gone or limited. There was a roughly 35 percent unemployment rate among blacks who were crowded into two sections of San Francisco.

However, we heard the city was working hard to restore business and housing opportunities, for blacks and other ethnic groups, to uphold its image as the most cultured and cosmopolitan city in the west.

As we toured the area, our favorite sights were the Fisherman's Wharf, with its charming vendors and the delightful smell of fresh steamed and fried seafood, historic Chinatown, the fabled cable cars slowly climbing the hills of the city, and those bridges, the likes of which I had never seen. The San Francisco – Oakland Bay Bridge, span across the bay to the city of Oakland, and the beautiful, red-orange colored Golden Gate Bridge rose above the San Francisco Bay Straight. It was also an exciting time to be in the Bay Area because there was so much buzz about Major League baseball moving to town, as the Giants and their star, Willie Mays "The Say Hey Kid" as he was affectionately called, were leaving the Polo Grounds in New York City after the 1958 season.

Eventually, we drove to Livermore to check out my new place of work, the Lawrence Radiation Laboratory. Once we arrived at the complex, I couldn't help but think how isolated and secure it appeared to be as my eyes panned the surrounding landscape. It was exciting to see the place I would start my career in technology, even though it was a long distance from San Francisco, and in the middle of nowhere. As we drove back to Delores' house, my wife and I realized that there may not be any living accommodations for black families in Livermore because of its remote location.

We were told to visit the city of Palo Alto, about 30 miles south of the city of San Francisco. As I drove south on Highway 101 and Bayshore Freeway, on my way to Blackwell Realty, I noticed that the fog bank disappeared as I passed the San Francisco airport. Then, as I drove farther south, I decided to exit Highway 101 at University Avenue, which led to Stanford University. My wife and I were immediately attracted to the beauty of the tree-lined streets. We had found an area that felt like a good place to look for an apartment or house. While driving around and enjoying the scenery, I realized I had lost my direction. So, I stopped at a service station to ask a middle-aged white gentleman for directions to Blackwell Realty. He responded, "I am sorry that I cannot help, but I suspect it is on the other side of Highway 101." Indeed, that realty company was in East Palo Alto. Still, as I think back, it was probably his way of saying that this was not the ideal location for me to be looking for real estate.

When we found Blackwell Realty, we sat down with an agent. After explaining our situation, we were told that restrictive covenants, prohibiting blacks and other people of color from living in certain communities, were placed on the deeds of homes in Palo Alto where we stopped to ask for directions, but that he knew of one community in East Palo Alto that would rent or sell to black families. At that point, I was thinking to myself, *we relocated to the West Coast, and we were still facing some of the same unequal treatment as we had experienced back home.* However, there was no turning back. I had to trust the decision I had made to take on a new life in California.

I'm usually a calm guy when it comes to big moments, but the night before my first day at the Lawrence Radiation Laboratory was different. I was quite excited but had never felt so nervous. To say I was uneasy and worried would be an understatement. I was thinking, *what if I fail and have to go back to Missouri with my tail between my legs.* I couldn't eat nor sleep, and breathing was hard, at times, that night. Virginia noticed it and said it was just a combination of anxiety and excitement. She said it was normal, especially after relocating to a new city and not knowing anyone I would be working with. She never mentioned that I may be nervous because I was black and would likely be working with almost all white males. Her words of encouragement made me realize that it was natural for a person in my situation to feel the anxiety.

I also thought about my mother telling me I had the ability to go as far as I wanted to go in life, but that it was up to me. After those relaxing thoughts, I managed to get a few hours of sleep. The next morning, after a hug, a kiss, and a coffee from Virginia, I was on my way to Livermore. I was even more excited to start my new job and prove my value.

The laboratory was run by the University of California for the United States Government. Naturally, I felt that it was extremely important work. From the very beginning, I was usually the first to arrive each morning and the last to leave each night. Some of the other workers were kind and seemed interested in finding out where I was from and how I had been selected for a position that was not usually filled by a black man or 'Negro' as we were called in 1958. It was also unusual to see a woman in that environment unless she was a secretary or typist. Some of the staff did not appear happy about me being there, but they would get over it eventually, as there were a couple other black men hired there over the next couple of years.

One colleague would often blame me for anything that went wrong in the office, from making mathematical miscalculations in a report to breaking a piece of office equipment or leaving cigarette ashes in an ashtray overnight. I never let it get to me because I knew that was how he wanted me to react. I just laughed it off inside and prayed for old crying Charlie, as I liked to call him. That was the name I used for him but only when I spoke about him to my wife, Virginia when she would ask me about my day. It seems that every other day I had something funny to tell her about ole Charlie. Many of my co-workers (all white in the beginning) defended me, and that was important as I went about my workdays. I stayed to myself mostly, focused on my work, and stayed true to my mother's advice to "give respect to get respect" and "learn as much as you can about everything that you can." The more I reflected on what my parents had instilled in me about fulfilling my dreams, the stronger I became. I didn't let it bother me that some of my co-workers were uncomfortable with me being there. I was not thrilled about working with some of them either, but I kept a poker face, most of the time, and never lost sight of my goal of being the best employee that I could possibly be. I could sense what I was up against from the very first day on the job. In hindsight, I may have learned to sense or read people from my poker-playing days back in St. Louis. You never know what can help you out in life. For me, it was the least likely of experiences, such as working in the craps room at the Kinloch pool hall, playing poker with that Jesuit Priest at SLU, and playing baseball with the older boys on those dusty fields when I was a kid. The most important thing I learned from those experiences was to be passionate and excellent at whatever I do and never accept failure as an option. And of course, I was hoping my mother's words of wisdom, "Don't let racism be a reason for not being successful," were going to help me out at that sometimes-lonely laboratory in Livermore. Somehow, I could hear my mother's words echoing all the way across the Oklahoma plains, the New Mexico mountains, and the Arizona desert, driving that message home in my mind.

Within five or six weeks after arriving in the Bay Area, we settled into our first home, an apartment in the Peninsula Gardens Area of East Palo Alto. It was a nice place but far from our dream residence. The neighbors were a good blend of people of color and white families. It was, literally, a melting pot. Most of the people were either enrolled in graduate and professional schools or beginning their careers like me. One of the neighbors and I became good friends and often talked about sports. We were both big fans of the San Francisco Giants. He also knew that my favorite team was the Los Angeles Dodgers, so he suggested we ride over to see the Giants play the Dodgers one Saturday afternoon. Jackie Robinson had retired by then, but I will never forget the fun we had watching Willie Mays patrolling centerfield as only he could do it. There was another Willie on the team as well. A big left-handed hitting rookie first baseman, Willie McCovey, hit a towering home run that day, as the Giants won easily over the Dodgers. The Giants finished third in the National League (NL) that year, behind the Braves and the pennant-winning Los Angeles Dodgers. Willie McCovey was selected as the league's Rookie of the Year. Three years later, the Giants took the NL Pennant but lost to those darn New York Yankees in the World Series. Following the Giants was a great way to relax and deal with the stress of the work week. I became a big fan over the years.

That year, Virginia began working as an electronics assembler. She did this for about six months to help us save some money. We decided, however, that the net material gains of her working full time were outweighed by the benefits of having a parent at home, especially being there when a child arrives home from school. I remembered my mother was always at home when I arrived from school and how much that meant to me as a young boy.

At the office, I continued to gain more knowledge about programming, a field that was growing by leaps and bounds at the time. I could foresee some great and innovative things were about to happen in that field, and I wanted to gain whatever competitive edge necessary to be a leader with this new technology. The highly specialized work dealing with radiation and nuclear energy at the laboratory needed these hi-tech programming skills, and I was fortunate to be a part of that movement. I simply outworked almost every one of my co-workers and gained the respect of my colleagues and management.

I was selected to work with the team responsible for the laboratory's most significant project at the time, which was to develop a software application that modeled the radiation diffusion that results from a nuclear bomb explosion. It was hard to believe I was working on something so big, something even I, with my limitless ambition, would never have imagined as a kid back in Kinloch. What we were doing had never been done before, and that was exciting. Yet, there were chilling thoughts that crossed my mind. I had harrowing notions of what it would look like if this model were ever truly tested, if a nuclear bomb were ever dropped somewhere, and the destruction that would occur in just a few explosive seconds. It was highly confidential work, so I could not discuss it outside the laboratory gates. That was okay with me because I enjoyed relaxing at home after work with my family. It was the perfect balance for work-related stress. I continued to spend quality time with family and enjoy other activities throughout my career.

I received recognition from my superiors, including Dr. Edward Teller, the Lawrence Laboratory Director himself, for my work and dedication on that project. I was considered a rising star at the Lawrence Livermore Laboratory. I was surely in the big leagues, as evidenced by another perk offered to me while working on this high-profile project. Since my supervisor knew about my difficult daily commute, he suggested I use a unique way of getting to work, on certain crucial days that required early arrival and late hours. He informed me that there was a helicopter leaving most days from a pad in Palo Alto. It was typically only used by higher-level management, but Dr. Teller had granted approval for me to use it on occasion until the project was completed. It was their way of showing appreciation for my work, and I was pleased by the offer. However, that commute by helicopter could potentially be a nerve-racking experience.

I closed my eyes and pictured myself parking the car, shielding my face and protecting my hat from the wind created by the force of the revolving chopper blades as I sprinted across the pad in my favorite business suit and boarded the aircraft in style just before liftoff. James Bond had not been created yet, but you get the picture. Only after I stopped daydreaming, the reality hit me, and all I could think of was how troubling this helicopter ride might be in bad weather, especially crossing the bay on dark, foggy mornings, my life flashing before my eyes, and imagining that aircraft going down and my family having to live without me. That worrisome thought didn't last long, though, and after a few commutes by helicopter, you couldn't tell me anything. I was no longer that poor little black kid from a segregated town in the Midwest. I was breaking barriers in a new field of technology and making some groundbreaking accomplishments, just like my mother said was possible. Now, I was thinking, *if only the boys back home at the pool hall could see me now.*

We were now in the 1960s, one of the most tumultuous decades in our history, marked by the civil rights movement, the Vietnam War, antiwar protests, political assassinations, and more. It could be said that January 20, 1961, was the dawn of a golden age in American politics with the inauguration of the confident and charismatic John F. Kennedy to our nation's highest office. It was also an indicator that technology would influence our lives in every way moving forward, as Kennedy's confidence and charisma were on display in the first-ever nationally televised presidential debate. His opponent, Richard Nixon, did not stand a chance in those debates, which clearly was an advantage for Kennedy. The television, now in many of America's households, had shown us how the advancement of technology would play a major role in politics and the exposure of contemporary issues throughout the decade.

The civil rights movement gained tremendous momentum during this period with the support of many celebrities, entertainers, and politicians, often witnessed in our living rooms from our black and white television sets. There were sit-ins at "Whites Only" lunch counters across the south, beginning with the Woolworth lunch counter sit-in by a group of North Carolina A&T students in Greensboro, North Carolina. I admired those young students for their bravery and strong beliefs that America must live up to the words it was founded on - *that all citizens shall have equal rights and freedom under the constitution.* Harriett Tubman once said, "Slavery is the next thing to hell." Quite frankly, I felt the segregation and discrimination my family and I had experienced so far in my life was not very far from the meaning of those words expressed by Tubman.

Most notable to me at this time was Dr. Martin Luther King, Jr, one of the greatest Americans who ever lived. He was able to use the optics of television to open the eyes of viewers around the world to the unfair and discriminatory treatment of black citizens across the nation, especially in the Jim Crow south. Despite the discrimination I faced, even in California, I was making progress, slowly, but surely. I was not being promoted as quickly as I thought I should, but I was respected at the Lawrence Laboratory for the quality of my work, so I believed that might help me in the future to be selected for a higher-level position. I kept thinking that we were not far from being truly free of discrimination, with President Kennedy leading our country and Dr. King speaking to America's conscience. It was my hope and dream to be in a great position to help bring new ideas to the field of computer programming and technology. My wife told me she had that dream often. With her envisioning big things for my future, and my desire to please her, I was always inspired to stay the course and be ready when the opportunity presented itself.

With our first child, Roy, Jr, approaching school age, Virginia began to investigate school districts. The Palo Alto Unified School District appeared especially attractive. I initially resisted moving to that area because of the difference in the cost of housing and other expenses.

We finally found a home in the Greenmeadow area in the southern part of Palo Alto in the later part of 1961, where we would live for almost 50 years. Developer Joseph Eichler built the development, which included 243 single-story modernist homes, in 1954 and 1955. We were able to select from six models, which they could modify at an additional cost. The homes' thin, lofty roofs and open, free-flowing interiors gave them a distinct look. The developer had already succeeded as one of the first developers to bring modernism to affordable single-family homes on the West Coast. The new Greenmeadow community represented the continuing refinement of his work. Along with his designers, Eichler built a reputation as an award-winning modern home designer. It was a beautiful home, and I promised Virginia that I wouldn't smoke my red label 'More' cigarettes in our new house. I must confess that on a few occasions, I had to sneak a puff or two.

In less than two years, five Black families, including mine, moved to that area. We had many family friends in the neighborhood, from black, white, and other ethnic groups.

We never really felt any sense of racism from any of the people in the neighborhood, and we built some close friendships with many of our neighbors who remained there for many years. The black families, however, all had a special bond, and they all had children close to the ages of our boys. We are still in contact with and close to many of them today, as well as other neighbors of the Greenmeadow community. Our family dentist, Dr. McKenna, lived at the end of our street and remained our family dentist for over 50 years. Dr. McKenna came to be our dentist when my youngest son, Chris, had all his front baby teeth accidentally knocked out while playing football with some of the bigger kids in the neighborhood. Dr. McKenna came to our house and comforted Chris, while he gently wiggled out the last couple of teeth that were still dangling from Chris's mouth. At that point, it was apparent that Chris was in good hands, and I knew from that moment on, Dr. McKenna had the comforting touch needed to manage our entire family's oral health.

Things were going so well for us in the Bay Area, but my father had taken ill back home, and I was on the phone with my mother more often as his health continued to decline. He passed away shortly afterward, and the hardest thing for me was that I did not get to be with him in his last days. We drove back to Kinloch to be with my mother and the rest of the family. It was the first time we had gone back home to Missouri. I knew the route, but it was more difficult this time. I had accomplished a lot in my career, as a husband,

and as a father, but I had never dealt with the death of someone so close to me. I kept my eyes on the road, but my mind occasionally wandered to the situation at hand. I had lost the man who taught me everything, from how to throw a curveball to how to treat a woman. The man whose work ethic I modeled. *What would I say to my mother when I arrived in Kinloch* was the question that consumed my thoughts and made Route 66 seem even longer than it had on our previous trip.

Once we arrived in Kinloch, and I saw the old house where I grew up, my memories of Daddy helping me into that ambulance when I was ten years old and cheering me on at those Sunday baseball games brought a smile to my face. That smile was probably Daddy's way of letting me know that he was okay and at peace – and that's what I whispered to my mother as I hugged her. The family spent valuable time that week remembering him for the wonderful father and husband he was, and we ensured Mother that we would be there for her. The homegoing service, held at our church in Kinloch, was attended by so many friends and family members. The pastor said some nice things about Daddy, and my mother wept. I know she felt blessed to have had Charles John Clay in her life, and in her mind, she would join him again someday. My siblings and I met a few times to make sure Mother had everything in order while I was there. Then it was back on the road to my new home – Palo Alto, California, but with Kinloch, and the love for my mother and father always in my heart.

Another year had come and gone. I had lost my dad, but there was so much to be grateful for. We were enjoying our new home, in addition to the Bay Area lifestyle. The new year had arrived, and we celebrated the new year the only way we knew how – that southern and mid-western way that my father would be proud of. Joyce and her new husband, Russ, joined us for the celebration. We listened to some good music, danced the night away, and dined on some chitlins, collard greens, and black-eyed peas for good luck. Virginia didn't eat chitlins, but she always cooked them for me. I remember always putting on a few pounds during the holidays from a few extra helpings of Virginia's soul food, but that year was memorable in so many ways.

In 1963, I decided that it may be a good time to move on from the laboratory as I had already experienced so much success there, and my value would be high if I tested the job market. It was also important for me now to be closer to home with Virginia being pregnant with our second child. I was particularly interested in a position that was open at the Control Data Corporation (CDC), so I applied and was selected for a management-level position with (CDC). It was bittersweet leaving the Lawrence Livermore Laboratory, the company that gave me an opportunity to move to California and where I cut my teeth, if you will. However, the CDC presented new challenges and growth in the technology field.

Soon after, my second son, Rodney, was born, bringing more joy to our home. Then Dr. Martin Luther King gave his inspiring "I Have a Dream" speech in Washington,

DC. On a sad note, President Kennedy was assassinated that November, which shocked the nation and had us all walking around in disbelief for days that felt like weeks. Kennedy's message was one of hope, especially for Black Americans, and now we were wondering if a southerner like Lyndon B. Johnson would step up from his position as Vice President and continue with Kennedy's plan to make civil rights a priority in his administration. The Vietnam War era was in full swing, which was another challenge for President Johnson. America continued to move forward, and LBJ, stood tall and led the way. He signed the Civil Rights Bill in July of 1964, with Dr. King and other civil rights leaders standing beside him. LBJ then successfully campaigned to become President for the next four years, starting in January of 1965. That was the year my youngest son, Chris, was born. Virginia and I had three sons, and she was the best wife and mother any man could ask for.

I made great strides at CDC, becoming known for my strong programming and management skills. The CDC was an emerging company, and I was thinking that it might be where my big break would come from. I was still writing home regularly to update my mother about my life in California and sending an occasional picture of the boys. At least once a month, I would make a telephone call to the family in Kinloch, but not more than that because long-distance calls were expensive before we had cell phones. I also bought another car later in the year. It was a black 63' Mercedes 190. I was earning more money at CDC, and I felt like rewarding myself for another accomplishment. I had achieved more than most men who looked like me, thanks to my angels, who continued to reassure me that there was always much more to achieve on this uncharted road to success.

The cover photo. I am programming a first-generation computer.

Chapter Six

HP DAYS

One day, in September 1965, while reading the Palo Alto Times newspaper, I discovered that the Hewlett-Packard Company (HP) was searching for a Software Development Manager. My curiosity was piqued because that was the title of the position I held at the computer manufacturer, Control Data Corporation (CDC). I read the job search material a week later and was curious enough to inquire as to why HP was engaging in such a search for a person with that title. You see, HP was known as a scientific instrumentation company at the time and not at all a computer company. Still, I wondered, could this be that big turning point in my career - the move that could propel me to something greater than I had ever imagined? David Jordan, an African American, who had also worked at Control Data, was now a personnel manager at HP. I inquired about the position with him, and he suggested that I apply, indicating that it may be a great opportunity. He also grilled me regarding my credentials and career goals on the day that I delivered my resume, and that helped me prepare for what could be a possible interview.

HP did invite me for an interview, which I accepted, simply to satisfy my curiosity. I pondered over it and felt that the process may be a waste of time for all parties, but when I gave it more thought, I decided to attend the interview. After spending five grueling hours with three interviewers, I asked to leave for the day, with the understanding that I would return the next day. The following day, I returned to continue the interview process, as I had promised. After four hours, I left with no answer regarding hiring status, convinced that there was no fit. However, within a few days, HP submitted an offer to me. I declined HP's offer because, in my opinion, HP was not as advanced in the computer industry. Besides, I was satisfied with my job at Control Data Corporation (CDC), where I gained a tremendous amount of knowledge about the industry.

In the end, HP invited me for another interview. This time, the interviewer was David Packard, Founder, and Chairman of the Board of HP. He was impressive and commanded attention from the moment he walked into the room. At about six-foot-five inches tall and athletically built, he looked the part of a guy who had participated in and won letters in football, basketball and track while studying at Stanford University, as I had been informed. After a firm handshake and direct eye contact, he moved a side chair closer and almost directly in front of me, which was a good sign. It was evident he wanted to make a deal with me, and my skin color did not matter to him at all.

Early in the interview, he mentioned that he was a big sports fan, and he asked if I had a favorite sport. Knowing that he liked sports, I answered, "Of course, my favorite is baseball, but I love competition, whether it is baseball, football, golf, shooting pool, or holding the winning hand in a poker game." His eyes seemed to light up, and he said something like, "I'm glad you mentioned that Roy, because I like managers who think that way. I'm the same way. I like to win. The way we handle business can often be relatable to sports and games. You know, sometimes it's necessary to take that extra base in baseball or call a timeout to draw up a special play in basketball when the game is on the line, wouldn't you say?" I quickly nodded in agreement. Mr. Packard continued, "That is the way I interact with my managers right here at HP." I leaned forward in my chair, only a few feet away, and said, "That is my management philosophy as well." He nodded his head in approval, paused, and then explained how he once set the Stanford school record for most points won by a freshman in a track meet. He seemed even more proud that he did it against the rival, UC Berkeley (Cal). It was obvious that the mental aspect of competitive sports was one of his favorite things to analyze and discuss, so I thought this Packard guy and I could get along.

During most of the interview, Mr. Packard described the purpose of the computer project. He informed me that

HP had bought the Dymec company outright in 1959, and it became the Dymec division of HP. He explained that he had also purchased Data Systems Inc. in 1964 and merged it into the Dymec Division. His goal was for HP to fully enter the computer business by 1966. He wanted to develop a computer to interface with HP test and measurement instrumentation to gather data and manipulate data acquired from those products. I told him it sounded like a brilliant idea.

Furthermore, he told me he could have bought Digital Equipment Corporation (DEC) for $25 million to accomplish his goal, but he chose to develop a computer from within HP. He explained that he wanted me to manage the computer systems software development. That interview with Packard changed my views about taking his position. I felt like I had just heard the infamous Notre Dame coach, Knute Rockne, deliver his "Let's do it for the Gipper" speech. David Packard had me ready to run into a brick wall at the end of that interview. He made me an offer, and I accepted it because I knew I would have an opportunity to lead the establishment of a new discipline within a well-established company. I would also have the full support of the company leader. I projected that we were about to create a business with a decades-long lead in the technology industry.

I have sometimes pondered why David Packard became personally involved in selecting me to be a trailblazer in the founding of computers by HP. Yes, I was knowledgeable, dependable, and a hard worker, which was all good, but it was evidently more than that. I discovered that David was a close acquaintance of Dr. Edward Teller, the "father" of the hydrogen bomb and the Director of Lawrence Livermore Radiation Laboratory. I came highly recommended by Dr. Teller, who always respected me for successfully developing the high-profile software product, FOLDERS (First Order Linear Differential Equations Resolution), which simulated radiation diffusion resulting from an atomic explosion. It was a great accomplishment and was listed in the software catalog at the radiation laboratory in Uppsala, Sweden.

The Hewlett-Packard computer division did not start in a garage in Palo Alto but rather in a trailer that was leased and placed on a parking lot of the HP Dymec Division, located at 295 Page Mill Road in Palo Alto. That is where I managed the first employees of the HP software group. I specified the products to be offered, and I designed and wrote some of the software. I was given authority to bring in the employees I needed, so I hired some programmers who had worked for me at CDC. I also recruited from the first graduating class of the Stanford University computer science program. The most gratifying part of the process came when I recruited several young graduates from Morehouse College, a historically black college (HBCU) in Atlanta, Georgia. Reaching back to find talent at HBCUs was something I repeated many times throughout my career. I later found out that David Packard was a strong advocate for expanding the pool of well-qualified talent by searching in previously overlooked minority talent pools. He was decades ahead of the push for "Diversity and Inclusion" that would come in the 2000s.

That was his general way of thinking, so I was very much operating as an extension of David, who I was now on a first-name basis with, and his goals to improve equality and opportunities for all in the workforce. We brought some very bright young professionals into the organization who just happened to be minorities. Those young people were excited about being a part of HP, and it was an exciting time indeed.

We made a site change as well. At one of our regularly scheduled review meetings, David asked, "How much space do you think you will need for the next 5 years?" I told him I would need 150,000 square feet. The corporate space acquisition manager, who was present and happened to hear the question, responded that he knew of a building of that size, which was new and unoccupied. David asked about the price and location of the building. The building was located in Cupertino, CA, on Wolfe Road, just off Hwy 280. The asking price was $5.2 million, but the owner, Varian, sought to sell due to some financial conditions. Packard responded immediately, agreeing that if that location was satisfactory to me, they would proceed and offer the asking price. The offer was made, and the transaction was completed within days. Along with the building, there were 32 acres of apricot orchards. The one condition that had to be resolved was that the previous owner lived on the parcel of land, and no further construction would be permitted if he was alive. We agreed to the owner's request because we had no plans for further construction at the time, and secondly, the owner was 92 years of age.

Therefore, my group became the first high-tech occupant in that part of Santa Clara County. That parcel of land is now the location of the Apple Computer "Spaceship" headquarters. One year after accepting the Hewlett-Packard position, I introduced a set of computer systems software comprised of operating systems and computer languages, which enabled the computer to be more user-friendly. The year was 1966 – which was ten years before Microsoft was founded. You see, Bill Gates was only 11 years of age when I introduced HP software. Shortly after I implemented the software, David Packard came to my office to tell me that he had designated me as one of the top 60 employees of the company, with all accompanying benefits, in perpetuity. Things were certainly working out for me.

When I told my wife what Packard had told me, she said, "I told you that was the dream that I had, and it is now coming true." We were so excited and wanted to celebrate, but it was a night with the boys, and they were too young to understand why we were so happy. All they wanted was Mommy and Daddy, so we ordered a pizza, opened a bottle of wine, and danced to our favorite song, 'Our Love Is Here to Stay,' all while looking over our shoulders and making sure everything was fine with Roy, Jr, Rodney, and Chris. I thanked Virginia for the dream and for her support and encouragement. It would be another early night for us, as

Virginia had the responsibility of getting Roy, Jr ready for school that next morning. I had to rest up and be prepared to lead my group at HP when the morning came. Before I fell asleep, I remember feeling blessed and fortunate to have a mother and a wife who never allowed me to make excuses or quit because of the color of my skin. They always told me I could do it. Maybe I was in the right place at the right time. Still, none of this would be possible without making the right decisions and being the right man for the job, a man with impeccable skills, an incomparable work ethic, and an incredible will to succeed against the odds.

We were highly respected in the hi-tech world, and the more we grew, the more respect Dave and I had for each other. Later, when he was being considered by President Nixon to become Deputy Secretary of Defense, he listed me as a reference. I was probably the first Kinloch, Missouri native to have that distinction, and I must say it was an honor to be involved in his vetting process.

I will never forget that otherwise usual Monday morning that caught me by surprise. While sitting at my desk and preparing for a staff meeting, I received an urgent phone call to report to the front office to meet with the FBI. Many thoughts ran through my mind as I approached that meeting. The FBI, I thought. Why would they want to speak to me? Suddenly, my breakfast was not agreeing with me as I spotted two well-dressed gentlemen, one balding, the other considerably younger, sitting together in the reception area. I stopped at the receptionist's desk, hoping she would let me know what was going on, but she simply nodded in the direction of the men who were now looking in my direction. I took a deep breath, walked over to them, and introduced myself. "Hello, I'm Roy Clay." We shook hands, and the agents, whose names I can't recall, cordially introduced themselves and showed their badges. I asked, "What can I do for you?" as I remained standing beside them. The older of the two said, "Mr. David Packard has been nominated for the position of Deputy Secretary of Defense, by President Nixon, and Mr. Packard has listed you as a reference, so we would like to ask you some questions sir." I promptly showed them to an adjacent conference room that was vacant. Once we were seated, they immediately asked questions, beginning with, "Do you think Mr. Packard is qualified to hold such a position, and will you tell us what you think of his management ability?" At that point, I breathed a huge sigh of relief and began to smile, and we all began to laugh. They could see that I was more at ease now, and after I responded to the first question, they fired away with some more personal questions about his character. They probably walked away thinking David could walk on water – and sometimes I felt that way about him myself.

David's choice to list me as a reference for the position showed the quality of respect he had for me. It also showed his substance as a person. He was a real man's man. However, it came as a loss to both of us in the end. I felt proud, especially as a young black man, at this time in America, to participate in David's selection for the Pentagon appointment. I was excited for him, but Dave leaving the building marked the beginning of the end of my HP career. The robust support he gave me was never matched while I was under the management of Bill Hewlett. Sometimes that happens in business, but you must work through it, and for the most part, we did. We both understood that I was Dave Packard's hire, and Bill and I would never have the bond that was there between David and myself. I still contend that the "Valley" would be known today as the "HP Valley", had my friend, David, not left HP to serve as a political appointee at the Pentagon.

I recall Bill Hewlett calling me one day to inform me that his son, Jim Hewlett, had just graduated from Yale with a degree in Math, and asked if I could possibly find a job for him. I agreed and asked that he send his son to see me. The meeting was short and sweet, and the hiring of Jim followed. As time passed and my group grew larger, I had a vision that to be successful, it would be necessary to create an environment conducive to creativity and productivity. One of my acts was to create a "flex-time" policy. An employee in my group, who was contracted to work an 8-hour day, and 40 hours per week, would have more flexible hours instead. I decided that the hours of greatest communication were between 10 am and 2 pm. Therefore, I asked that everyone be in the office between those hours, to avoid having trouble with scheduling meetings. The remaining hours worked were at the discretion of each individual employee.

There was an incident that threatened the success of my new idea. Mr. Hewlett called to inform me that his son told him that he did not report to work until 9 o'clock or later some days because he would sometimes play golf beforehand. I sensed right away that this was not going to be a very friendly phone call. Hewlett was clear, "Without exception, an HP employee should report to work at 7:45 am, take a coffee break between 9:35 am and 9:45 am, take lunch between 11:45 am and 12:30 pm, take a coffee break between 2:35 pm and 2:45 pm, and leave work at 4:30 pm." I simply hung up the phone without giving him a definitive response. The next day, I told Jim about the conversation, to which he responded, "Darn-it, my father and I had not talked much recently, and I thought I would break the silence by describing how much I enjoyed the work environment that you had established, but I will not speak about it again." The conversation with Jim was brief, but I did manage to encourage him that it would be a good idea to communicate more with his father. He continued to work for my group as a software developer, along with the other exceptional professionals in my group. He was very productive and appeared to like his work, but he told me he had no interest in becoming a corporate manager. I guess he did not want the pressure of trying to follow in his dad's footsteps at that time. He was more of a laidback kind of guy and preferred a more relaxed environment, which is why he liked my management style.

I continued with the implementation of "flex-time," and it was a huge success with my group. In fact, when word got around in the industry about my "flex-time" approach to managing my employees, I started to get calls from many professionals in the field who were looking for new job opportunities. It made recruiting excellent employees a lot easier. However, I am not sure if my "flex-time" idea would have worked without young Jim praising it as much as he did when he discussed his work with his father.

My managerial influence at HP can be measured by the following situations that I think convinced Bill Hewlett that my style of management was a benefit to the company. Several months later, Bill Hewlett called me at 9 o'clock on a Saturday night to inform me that the system had shut down while he was working on his computer at his home. I called the Cupertino facility, and one of my employees responded, informing me he had taken the computer down for maintenance. Additionally, he was surprised that someone was using it on a Saturday night, but he said he would put the computer back on the air. I called Hewlett back to inform him what had occurred. I reminded him that one of the benefits of flextime was having the flexibility to work late or on the weekend as he was doing. He said that it was a point well taken.

Flexible work hours slowly became a part of the culture at HP while I was there, as evidenced by an article I read a couple of years after I had left HP. It stated that HP had invented "flextime." Another situation that was quite comical occurred when Hewlett called to inform me that a programmer was seen walking through the factory on his way to the restroom wearing sandals. He asked that I prevent anyone from walking through the factory without wearing steel-toed shoes in the future. Hewlett was a great and brilliant manager, by all respects, but I did not always agree with him, and this was another one of those times. I responded by saying it would cause very little pain to have a piece of software fall on someone's foot. I explained that we were talking about programs, procedures, and routines associated with the operation of a computer system and not the actual hardware, which made up the physical components.

Situations like these explain the atmosphere that prevailed during my beginning days at HP, at a time when I worked as much as 13 hours day, as I was often reminded by my wife. Those long, dedicated hours were spent managing, specifying, designing, implementing products, and always recruiting skilled young talent. I knew the magnitude of the job that I had to do, but I had no one with whom I could discuss issues after David left the company. Fortunately, two things happened. Hewlett gradually became a fan and saw that I was doing some great things with my group over time. Also, Tom Perkins, who eventually became a very close associate of mine, was named General Manager of the first Computer Division of HP. Tom Perkins elevated my position to HP Director of Research and Development, with oversight of all our company's computer products.

In that role, I reported directly to Mr. Perkins. My first act was to extend an offer to an IBM employee to become Manager of Computer Development. The offer was accepted by the candidate, but Hewlett interceded. He did not want to hire anyone at that high level from outside HP. Hewlett was loyal to our employees, so I rescinded the offer. At Hewlett's request, we hired a long-time HP manager, Dick Hackborn. Incidentally, sometime later, Hackborn became the Chairman of the Board at HP. He ultimately hired Carly Fiorina as Chief Executive Officer (CEO) of HP. Fiorina was an outsider at the time of her selection as CEO. That position was five management levels higher than my original offer to the IBM manager so that conflicted with the guidance I was given when I tried to hire an outsider from IBM. Given the direction HP was heading at the time, having lost the direction of the original founders Hewlett and Packard at the time of Fiorina's hiring, an outsider was probably what the company needed. There is more background on that transitional period in the history of HP, in the book, The HP Way, written by David Packard.

Tom Perkins and I had grown closer by this time, and it was obvious that he was a rising superstar in the industry. Little did I know at the time how big a role Tom and I, by association, would have in the evolution of Silicon Valley. As evidenced by the following anecdote that I will share from Tom's book, Valley Boy. As the story goes, Tom was the GM of the team that I managed, the software development team. One day he was running a team meeting, and a manager from another group tried to pull me out of that meeting to attend another meeting. Tom refused to let me leave the meeting. This manager was furious, so in retaliation, he had Tom's company-issued Buick taken away from him for not letting me leave his meeting. The angry manager was not Tom's boss, but he did have the authority to approve the issuance of company cars. By that time, Tom was already independently wealthy from another venture outside of HP. The brash guy that Tom was, he went out and bought a Ferrari to drive to work, just to annoy the guy who had his company car taken away. Tom never seemed to let anything get him down – but I guess it helps when you have the kind of wealth he had. I never forgot what he did for me that day. It was great to have a guy like that in my corner.

Tom was wealthier than anyone I knew, and while I was at HP, he invited me and Virginia to cruise on his multimillion-dollar yacht. He and his wife, Gerd, also hosted my 40th birthday party in Edinburgh, Scotland, at an amazing place called the Littlefield House. Imagine that. That's pretty good for a guy who grew up in a poor little segregated town in the Midwest. After that trip is when Tom elevated me to General Manager of the Computer Division at HP. I continued working in the "HP Way" and its environment that I knew so well because I helped create it. Serving as the General Manager of the Computer Division, I built a solid relationship with Tom Perkins. However, I could feel that change was coming our way. The handwriting on the wall, that Hewlett was going to take the computer division in a different direction, came a couple of months earlier when Hewlett ordered the team to cancel a deal made with Holiday Inn. The deal was for a significant number of computers to be used for business computing. One of our sales and marketing whiz kids, Jimmy Treybig, a few others who helped close the deal, and I were all shocked and saddened.

The final straw, which signaled the end of my HP tenure, came one unsuspecting day in June of 1971 when Bill Hewlett came to visit me at my office. He began a conversation by congratulating me for the fine job I had done as interim General Manager of the HP Computer Division. Then he announced an increase in my salary. I thanked him very much. Next, he announced that he was granting me a new series of stock options. I again thanked him. Then came the blockbuster from Hewlett, "I have decided to name someone else as the new permanent General Manager of the Computer Division as I want someone to manage the Computer Division who has no computer knowledge." At that point, the meeting ended without much else being said by either of us. I think he saw the shock and appearance of sheer puzzlement on my face. I had no words, at least none that I could utter at any place other than maybe the pool hall back home in Kinloch.

Many thoughts ran through my mind as I stood there in disbelief after Bill Hewlett walked away that day. The thought I remember most vividly was, did he just tell me that he did not want a computer division within HP, after all the effort we had made to move HP forward in that industry.

That division had been my baby from the beginning. As a matter of fact, some say I was its godfather - the person most responsible for that division's culture and success. What was once a team was about to become a broken home; it was like waking up from a good dream gone bad.

The conclusion that I obviously reached was that my career at HP was over. I went home shortly after that and mentioned the context of the meeting to my wife. Without hesitation, she responded, "Give your resignation immediately; as bright as you are, and as hard as you work to succeed, you will do well at whatever you choose. I will support whatever you choose to do." Once I realized I had Virginia's support, I submitted my resignation the next day. I left the company two weeks later, on July 1, 1971. I'm not saying this was an easy decision, as I considered HP to be like family after the opportunity Dave Packard had given me. Still, I knew it was time to move on, and coincidentally, Bill Hewlett's son, Jim, left the company a few months after I departed.

My angel, Virginia, always stood by my side through it all and urged me to take advantage of this situation as an opportunity to achieve more than before. It was important for me to hear that from her. It was also important to spend more time with my sons and realize how much they were growing up right before my eyes. Rodney and Chris were in school now, and Roy Jr, was already in middle school. We had always spent Saturday evenings going bowling as a family and playing catch in the yard, but now I was appreciating it more. It was a joy to sit with Roy, Jr, while he played the piano. He was a natural musician, and I was glad we had invested in a piano for our home when he was nine years old. In four years, he had become a featured artist in school musical events. He also had excellent math skills, and now I had more time to help him with his math homework. He recently told me that during his early teen years, I explained the connection between music and mathematics to him. Those early discussions helped him excel at both. I will take the credit, but honestly, I think Junior was just a natural. Spending time with Virginia and the boys was as much fun as it was important. I also had entrepreneurial visions and thoughts on my mind, which were driving me toward greater paths.

Chapter Seven

THE DAWN OF "SILICON VALLEY"

To the best of my hazy recollection, the first time I gave any real thought about how I wanted to be remembered was while taking an early evening summer walk less than a mile from my home, only days after I left Hewlett Packard in 1971. I found myself resting on an old rusty bench at the Cubberley High School ballfield. It was the same field where I had spent countless hours coaching my son Rodney. He was quickly becoming a very skilled five-tool baseball player. However, there were no loud cracks of the bat or thuds of the ball pounding my mitt this day. No sir. I was alone, hoping to clear my mind, just a few steps from the batting cage. As I relaxed there, in my favorite lightweight black and white jogging suit, I found myself contemplating, not about the joy of America's pastime, hotdogs, or apple pie, but about what my family and I had experienced over the last few years, and whether I had fulfilled my purpose up to this point. Then I pondered about what I should do next.

Would I get through this challenging career-changing phase and have success as an entrepreneur? During my time working for HP, we experienced so many highs and lows in America, and I reflected on some of those historical moments this early August evening to get a better sense of moving forward. It was just me and my thoughts, shielded from everything else by the vast field of freshly mown grass and occasional whir of a car driving down Nelson Drive, a street that bordered the field.

As I gazed into the sunset beyond the outfield fence, I thought about how our nation had gained civil rights and voting rights legislation and how we lost two giants, Dr. Martin Luther King, Jr, and presidential candidate Robert F. Kennedy, who were both tragically assassinated. My eyes misted over a little as I remembered living those tragic moments of 1968 and viewing the news footage of both men being brazenly shot down for no reason other than them wanting to make our country live up to its constitutional promises. I remembered the riots, the violence, and "Soul Brother" signs in storefront windows, in the aftermath of the Dr. King assassination, and the tears and sadness when we lost Kennedy. "Liberty and justice for all" was now just a whisper after those notable voices had been silenced. Soon we would send men to the moon, but there were protests and acts of civil unrest here on the ground.

I realized how fortunate I was that there were not many racial incidents in my community, or at least that I was aware of personally. The most annoying thing I experienced was being pulled over quite a few times, without cause by the police, to check my driver's license and vehicle registration. That is something most Black men had to tolerate back then, especially when driving a nice car, such as my cherished black Mercedes 190 in a community like Palo Alto. That has always been par for the course when you are driving while black. Somehow, I always stayed calm and hoped that those white officers would change their ways before long, especially since my young sons would be driving someday as well. I had survived that encounter with police in Ferguson, Missouri when I was a teenager and I never wanted that to happen again to me nor did I want my boys to experience it either.

As this contemplative mood continued, a positive memory of the great Aretha Franklin came to mind as I took in the calmness that surrounded me on that ballfield. I thought back to a day in 1966 when Virginia and I saw Aretha perform at a sold-out Oakland Coliseum. We had a fun time that night. We were both wearing blue that night as we stepped into the arena's main lobby dressed to the nines, as we always did when going out for events. I always said, looking good was part of it. We loved the song "Respect" written by Otis Redding in 1965, and although Aretha did not record it until 1967, she sang it that night, much to our delight. The lyrics were powerful and made me think of my mom's words about giving respect to receive respect, so it became one of my favorite songs from that moment on. I remember the arena was rocking unforgettably, with Aretha lovers of all shapes, sizes, and colors filling the aisles and seats.

Aretha Franklin also influenced us in another way. After that concert in 1966, we decided to buy a piano and get Roy, Jr into the piano lessons. Within a couple of years, Roy actually became a better pianist than his teacher. How often have you seen that before? Maybe some of that Aretha Franklin magic at her concert rubbed off on my oldest boy, in some mysterious way.

After all that reminiscing at the ball field, I stood up, stretched, and quickly made my way home. When I arrived at the house, I felt rejuvenated the rest of the evening. I'd say there is undoubtedly something about sitting at a park all alone and deep in thought that truly clears the mind. Now, all I was thinking about was getting my consulting business solidly off the ground and continuing to make a difference in the world of computer technology, an industry I had helped to father and build from the very beginning of my move to the Bay Area. It seemed increasingly evident that I was in the middle of something that could continue to change humanity, and I was excited and eager to get my company started.

I sat down and had dinner with the family and realized how fortunate I was to have Virginia, my three sons, and ambitious plans for a bright future. I also concluded that I had an opportunity to help people who needed a voice like mine. My voice was not melodic like Aretha's. However, it was that of a man who had experienced inequality and deprivation and still succeeded, despite the odds. I only hoped that my voice would always resonate my empathy, understanding, and heartfelt concern for others. Later that night, I whispered to Virginia that I had been thinking about my legacy. She smiled, snuggled against me, and said, "You're a great man, Roy." I looked back at her and said, "We're great together."

A week later, I did something I had not done before. I flew home to Missouri for the first time. I had decided there would be no more driving that far for the Clays. My mother had never stepped foot on California soil, so I thought this would be the right time for me to visit her and then bring her back to spend time with us, especially since I was told that mom was showing some signs of declining health. Flying in an airplane was not exactly on her bucket list, but after a little coaxing, she did fly back to stay with us for a few weeks. We enjoyed her company, and she was amazed with our home and the Bay Area. She kept saying that things were so strange out west and that it felt like she was in a foreign country. When we assured her that she was still in America, she chuckled and said, "Maybe so, but it's not the America I know." I said, "Mom, it's more like America than you know, trust me." More than anything, she just couldn't get used to us having white neighbors living next door. Before mom returned home, she told me she was proud of all that I had achieved despite the obvious obstacles. I told her that I had followed her advice of not letting anything keep me from being successful. I thanked her for those words of wisdom and assured her that my best was still ahead.

During the last quarter of 1971, I founded my own technology business consulting firm. Operating as Roy L. Clay and Associates, I leveraged so much of what I learned during my years at HP, Control Data, and Livermore to provide consulting that specialized in identifying and nurturing prospective investments in computer technology start-ups for Tom Perkins' company, Kleiner Perkins, the world's premier technology-focused venture capital firm and the true catalyst of Silicon Valley as we know it today. Three of those investments - Tandem Computers, Compaq, and Intel – have combined valuations, as of 2021, nearing $1 Trillion.

I have my wife Virginia to thank for my business success. She reminded me of a quote by Dr. Martin Luther King, Jr that was very inspirational. King wrote, "If you can't fly, run. If you can't run, walk. If you can't walk, crawl, but by all means, keep moving." This is an example of how she encouraged me to go into business for myself after I decided to leave HP. Her support of me when I was down helped me think clearly and confidently about moving forward and not letting a disappointment stop me during that challenging time in my career.

I wasted no time opening my first office, in a premier location, on University Avenue in downtown Palo Alto. It was an excellent place to grow my company. I hired several new employees in my first year as the business grew faster than I had imagined. It was no surprise that I had to look for a new and larger space in that building, but I was not complaining. It was clearly a sign that I had made the right decision.

I brought the wisdom and knowledge that I gained as a manager at HP into my new business. Primarily, "Build a quality product and charge a commensurate price." It's as simple as that. That is the basis of business, and when you keep it that way, you have a much greater chance of success. And oh yes, I never forgot my mother's words, "Give respect to get respect." I realized, early, that being respected and caring about others in the industry, as well as in my community, was how I wanted to be remembered, along with operating the best business this side of the Mississippi of course.

It was also important to me to reach back and bring other minorities into the industry and guide them along the way. Several of the bright young people I brought into the company were from HBCUs. They were graduates of Morehouse (Atlanta, GA) and Wilberforce (Ohio), as I recall. A few were from Stanford, which was nearby. Some of our staff meetings had the appearance of a melting pot, with all colors of people, and a few women too, which made us unique. As a result of the various backgrounds of our employees, many new ideas were expressed and presented in our meetings. Diversity and inclusion were not popular topics of discussion in the Bay Area in the early 1970s, but it happened naturally within my company. I thought, *if I didn't hire minorities, who would?* I also remembered how David Jordan helped me when I was hired by HP. Now, it was my chance to help people who were similarly situated and who did not usually get this kind of opportunity. It was an opportunity to bring some brilliant young minds into the rapidly growing hi-tech industry.

I played chess, bridge, table tennis, golf, and participated in many things of interest with my employees. I also made it a point to create an atmosphere in my workspace that was conducive for an employee to be as creative and productive as possible. That atmosphere included giving respect to them as individuals and enabling each person to create his or her workspace, including choosing the time for most productive work.

I still think the friendship and advisory relationship that I had with Tom Perkins was the primary factor in the development of my entrepreneurial career. While we were at HP, Tom became familiar with my professional skills, managerial ability, and vast knowledge and advisory skills in computer technology. He always felt comfortable with me around, and he knew that I respected him as much as he respected me. There were never any hidden agendas between us. This bond was so relaxed that we sometimes got together after work to discuss strategies and just *shoot the breeze.* Tom was much more adventurous than I was, so Virginia wasn't thrilled about me spending time with him, but she never made a big deal about it since Tom had become my biggest supporter. Besides, she realized that having an occasional cocktail together while discussing the latest in the high-tech industry was part of building business relationships.

I recall saying to Virginia, "Tom is no different from me; he's just tall, white, and rich." We both looked at each other, I smiled, and she laughed. We realized at that very moment that those were typical characteristics of what success looked like in the business world - a microcosm that I had somehow penetrated. That was interesting to think about as I looked towards the sky, literally and figuratively, for an answer to why I had just discovered the stark contrast in the lives Tom and I had ascended from. It was like part right out of Dickens' *A Tale of Two Cities*. I looked back at Virginia, and while still chuckling, she said, "One thing that is similar is how you both command attention when you enter a room." She hugged me and I said, "Success does get attention." She replied, "Your success is more impressive though." Instantly, I knew she was referring to something from Frederick Douglass that reads, "You are not judged by the height you have risen, but from the depth you have climbed." Indeed, I had come a long way from where my journey had begun.

It was a fascinating time period in the Valley, a place that was fast becoming known as "Silicon Valley," thanks in large part to the innovations and investments being driven by Kleiner Perkins. Earlier that year, journalist, Don Hoefler, used it as the title of a series of articles, "Silicon Valley USA," for a weekly trade newspaper named Electronic News, which started early in 1971. The word silicon comes from the primary sand-like material and silicon transistors found in modern microprocessors. Like most technological terms, it evolved and stuck around. As more tech companies called this South San Francisco Bay Area region their home, it continued to grow into a global center of technological innovation and entrepreneurial spirit. Thus, the name, Silicon Valley, was born. Palo Alto, my home, was right in the middle of this technology business boom. I had always called it "the valley," so within months I was comfortable with the new term for our region. All the while, I kept thinking, *with all this money flowing into "the valley," is this the tech version of the California Gold Rush all over again?* Quickly the area was becoming known for technology-based wealth. This was the time to be an entrepreneur in Palo Alto. This was my time, and I did not hesitate to take the ball and run with it.

Intel was founded in Mountain View, California, by Robert (Bob) Noyce and Gordon E. Moore, in 1968. Noyce was a physicist and co-inventor of the integrated circuit, while Moore, a chemist, was known for "Moore's Law." Both men left Fairchild Semiconductor to create Intel. Many Silicon Valley start-ups had fabled origins in a youthful founder's garage, but Intel was different. Intel opened its doors with $2.5 million in funding arranged by Arthur Rock, the American financier who created the term venture capitalist. Intel's founders were middle-aged technologists who had already established their reputations. Noyce was one of the co-inventors of the silicon integrated circuit, about nine years earlier, when he was the general manager of Fairchild Semiconductor, a division of Fairchild Camera and Instrument.

My team and I met with Bob Noyce just prior to the 1971 release of their first microprocessor, the Intel 4004 Microprocessor. Robert was one of my first clients when I started my consulting business. He met with me several times in my company's office on University Avenue in downtown Palo Alto to discuss the design of the chip and how best to market it. Each time he and his team visited; he brought several chip prototypes. Initially, the Intel team wanted to build devices in which the chip would be used, but after several conversations and research, I advised him to first concentrate on selling the chip – thus helping shape Intel's business model as we know it today. Although Intel created the world's first commercial microprocessor chip in 1971, the chip was not extraordinarily successful until the breakthrough of the personal computer (PC). When computers became more popular in the late 1970s, the sales of Intel's microprocessor skyrocketed in the early 1980s.

The microprocessor represented a significant advance in the technology of integrated circuitry. It miniaturized a computer's central processing unit, making it possible for small machines to perform calculations, which in the past, only exceptionally large machines could do. Major technological innovation was needed before the microprocessor could become the basis of what was first known as a "mini-computer" and then familiar as a "personal computer." Intel also created one of the first microcomputers in 1973 after opening its first international manufacturing facility in 1972 in Malaysia, which hosted multiple Intel operations. They would go on to open assembly facilities and semiconductor plants in Singapore and Jerusalem in the early 1980s, and manufacturing and development facilities in China, India, and Costa Rica in the 1990s. I actually traveled to Malaysia as part of my work with Intel after they opened the facility there.

Once I get started, I'm hard to stop. Most of my siblings, who have all gone on to glory now, were like that too, I suspect, as many of them had businesses of their own. Charles had a side real estate business while working first for Ford and then General Motors in Detroit. My oldest sister, Pauline, had a shoe store that she ran out of my parent's basement, and my youngest brother, William, was an expert carpenter and had a contracting business in Alaska when they were developing the pipeline. He also flew airplanes while he was there. The Clays have always been some industrious and high-energy people. As my mother would say, "We come from good stock."

When I visited my mother in 1972, it was more evident that her health had declined a bit. She was just shy of four scores now, and sometimes she had a hard time remembering the boys' names. It's difficult to accept seeing a parent that way, but there were other times she was just as sharp as ever. I felt terrible that I was not there with her during her last years. Thankfully, some of my siblings gave her the attention she deserved. I hope she felt the love and appreciation I had for her. I owed her that and more for making me into the man I had become, but I realized some things can never be paid back in full. Sometimes you must pay up in other ways. I hoped I would find those other means of showing my appreciation, someday, for all she had given me.

One way to show my appreciation for all that my parents had done for me was to continue being the best husband and father I could be. I occasionally gave guest lectures to my sons' school classes about computers. As a family, we spent a lot of time bowling, starting in about 1966. I was blessed with the ability to excel at most sports and activities, so I coached my boys on the basic elements of the game. I even teamed up with my oldest son, Roy, Jr, in adult-junior leagues bowling for a few seasons. Roy, Jr continued bowling for many years, competing in semi-pro leagues in the Bay Area in later decades.

While we were on a family trip to St. Louis, I took the boys by the pool hall in Kinloch, where I worked as a teenager. That's where I taught them the basics of pool, and they loved the game. I bought a pool table for our house as soon as we returned to Palo Alto, and they continued playing regularly. I taught Junior how to play table tennis, and he won several local tournaments. Rodney played for several little league baseball teams and was an all-star player. Chris started playing soccer in elementary school and played every year into his teen years. My boys were fulfilling some of my childhood dreams to participate in outstanding leagues and competitions that were not available to me. It was cathartic for me to see them excel at games that I played well but never had a chance to compete in at a high level. I was happy that my dreams were coming true through them. It was important to be there for them at as many of their games and practices as possible. Sure, I was often tired, and I struggled many mornings to get out of bed, but I did it because I had to. I owed it to my sons, and I wanted to be a good example to other fathers.

Family and community were vital to both Virginia and me. We had monthly barbeques at our home with our family, neighbors, and some of our close friends we had met since moving to the Bay Area. Friends and colleagues like the Greens, Boyds, Walkers, Lockharts, and many others showed up often to the backyard get-togethers. They were primarily young black professionals who took parenting and their careers seriously. They had children who were very smart and talented – many of them went on to do remarkable things. One of the best things about living in Palo Alto was that the schools were excellent and rated highly. For that reason alone, I felt that choosing to move there was the best decision we ever made.

As my business was growing exponentially, I heard of a situation over in East Palo Alto where there was a lack of funding for the local Boys' Club, which meant that the kids in that city, most of them black and from lower-income families, would be deprived of some opportunities that were available to young people in surrounding jurisdictions. I decided to get involved because I was one of those children when I was a young boy. I grew up poor and wished that I had a club or little league team that I could have played for and participated in like the kids in Ferguson. This advocacy work for the city of East Palo Alto, which was only separated from Palo Alto by a freeway, was natural for me. I had always volunteered my time in the valley as a member of the Palo Alto YMCA Board of Directors; the Executive Board of the Stanford Area Council Boy Scouts; the Palo Alto-Stanford United Fund; the Advisory Committee to the Flint Center for Performing Arts; and as a Palo Alto Little League baseball coach. I was also a member of the Palo Alto Medical Foundation Board of Directors, which would turn out to be a game-changer in later years.

Eventually, I was asked by some of my colleagues and friends to run for the Palo Alto City Council. I had never attended a City Council meeting or hearing before, much less run for any office in the past. However, the city needed black representation on the City Council, and I was told that I was the man who could win. I had no political past, and I was an entrepreneur and well-liked in the community. I cared about my city and its people, so I thought, why not. After a short campaign and learning everything about my city, the election had come and gone. With the help of my friends and my wife and sons, I won the election. It was another accomplishment for me that was unlikely, but now it was time to work for the people who supported me. It was time to fulfill my promises. It was 1973, and I was the first African American elected to the Palo Alto City Council.

Built in 1965, the Palo Alto City Hall was a 15-story modernism-style building. I always admired the structure and its beautiful grounds, and now it would be like home to me for the next four years. I was asked several times if being the first would bring added pressure to the position, but I did not look at it that way. Since my days at St. Louis University and throughout my entire professional career, I had dealt with similar situations, and I never shied away from them before. Therefore, I was once again up for the challenge. I knew everyone would be watching, so I made sure I walked into city hall in a good-looking suit, with a confident stride, and a little "swagger," as the young fellows say now. I always admired the late Sidney Poitier's confident style after watching him in the movie, *To Sir with Love,* so why not emulate him.

In my first years being the only Black councilperson, I was mistaken a few times to be someone's chauffeur. Then there were the times when I was told by city hall employees that only city officials were allowed on the floor where the City Council meets. I also got accused of parking in the city council members' parking lot by police officers. In each case, I politely let these people, who were profiling me based on race, know who I was without causing a scene. I even slipped them a few of my business cards that included my picture and asked for their future support. I thought that might help them remember that there was now a Black man sitting on the city council. I'm not sure what they did with those cards or whether they ever supported any of my policies. Still, it sure was satisfying to see the humbled and embarrassed looks on some of their faces as I walked away with a wide smile of genuine pride and enjoyment.

This went on for months, but that comes with being the first. I had broken another barrier where African Americans had not been before. Every time I walked into that building or was mentioned in the newspaper, I realized it gave a lot of people, who looked like me, a sense of pride that is only understood by those who are deprived or underrepresented. There is something about seeing someone like you in a position that you never dreamed was possible before. I felt like a celebrity when I walked down the hallways of city hall. The smiles and handshakes, from black men and women, were priceless. I can only imagine they felt anything was achievable in public office, and otherwise, after seeing me holding down that position with class and respect.

One day, as I left the building early to attend a meeting, I greeted a young woman as she was ascending the front steps, not knowing that she would become a lifelong friend and supporter. I had just given handshakes to two building custodians, as I did every day. People say I was kind to everyone, but it was important to be approachable and down to earth with all our constituents, regardless of their walk in life. The polite young black woman with a medium-length afro hairstyle, who I approached on the outside stairs leading to the main entrance, was surprised that I spoke to her. I introduced myself and asked how her day was going. She said, "Hello, I'm Gloria Young. It has been a busy day running some errands with my husband. Now I'm returning to my office where I am an assistant to the City Clerk, Anne Tanner." I informed her that I was an acquaintance of Ms. Tanner, and that I was a member of the city council. I asked her to contact me if I could ever help her with her career. I gave her my card. She thanked me, and as I walked away, I told her to contact me if she was interested in networking once a month with other black professionals. She did just that and attended the next meeting at Ming's, a hip local establishment in Palo Alto.

She became a regular member of the group after a few meetings, and when she realized that I was the leader of those networking/mentoring sessions, she asked if she could assist me in organizing the events. I agreed, and I also became a mentor to Gloria. She soon became friends with my wife, Virginia as well. Gloria had a young son with severe disabilities and considered Virginia and me to be her advisors on matters dealing with her son. She noticed Virginia's mothering skills with our boys and proclaimed that Virginia had mother's wit. She has remained friends with my boys and me through the years. As unassuming as she was when I spoke to her on those city hall steps, it was the right thing to do. She would go on to do great things and be a shining light in the Palo Alto city government – and I had gained a daughter as well.

While balancing my time between my city council, business, and family responsibilities, I was a contributor when Tandem Computers got its start in 1974. Another former HP computer division employee was Tandem's founder, but the initial venture capital investment in Tandem Computers came from my friend, Tom Perkins. Tom's firm, Kleiner Perkins (KP) created their own startups, which was a major factor in the rapid growth of Silicon Valley, and the first large investment was with Tandem Computers. My company, Roy L. Clay and Associates, had provided consulting services to Tom and his KP team from the beginning. Now, our role was to work with Tom to help develop the technology and market plan for Tandem computers. Tandem was soon the dominant manufacturer of fault-tolerant computer systems for ATM networks, banks, stock exchanges, telephone switching centers, and similar commercial transaction processing applications requiring maximum uptime and zero data loss.

Tandem Computer went on to become KP's first high-tech investment to go public. The more quality consulting my company and I provided to KP, the more senior-level positions I was offered by the companies who were KP clients. The offers were substantial, but in keeping with my commitment to being a family and civic-minded person, I declined those high-ranking positions so I could spend more time with my family and work in the valley on civic and charitable activities. It was also vital for me to continue developing young talent, especially minorities and women, by offering positions within my business, one of only a handful of companies founded by an African American in the early days of what is now Silicon Valley.

My friend, Gloria Young, was helping me with the many issues and projects that had concerned me from the time I set foot in that City Hall building. I spent a massive amount of time looking out for my city and helping others, especially young people of color who finally had someone who genuinely had their backs. She also moved into a higher position in the City Clerk's office. She was growing professionally, and folks were taking notice. Most of the black professionals that met at Ming's had technology backgrounds or were trying to break into that field. Many evenings, the tab was on me because I wanted them there mingling at Ming's, if you will, and able to fully take in my story and career advice. The industry was still new to everyone, not just minorities, so this was a good time to help all young people learn more about technology careers. I was hiring more minorities than anyone else, and Gloria complimented me for that. She and another friend, Ken Coleman, always said it was because of the struggles I experienced in segregated little Kinloch, Missouri, that I was in such a space to give back. I continued bringing others into this early era of Silicon Valley, and I established the Friday Night Breakfast Club, which was a more formal networking and social organization aimed at nurturing and connecting young black male and female professionals who were interested in technology and other fields that were underrepresented in the Bay Area. I never said "never" when it came to helping others. It was just in my blood.

The weeks, months, and years passed swiftly while I was a council member. Then in 1976, I was voted by my colleagues on the council, to become the city of Palo Alto's first black Vice Mayor, and I served in that position from 1976 to 1977, all while still maintaining my company. I thought about saying no, but why stop when you are making a positive impact and having fun. There was simply no rest for the weary and sleep-deprived, so I was ready to work as soon as I was sworn in. The swearing-in ceremony was very emotional for my family and me. Virginia and I held hands a lot that day as we reflected back to our humble beginnings, wedding day, and first big leap when we drove to California, with only a job offer and a dream to hang onto. The boys were sharp that day, and rightly so as the newspaper and television news cameras were there to capture history being made. From the beginning of my term as a city council person, my priorities had always been dedication to open space, which was Palo Alto's mark of distinction, so I continued with that agenda and other pressing issues that were important to our city. I wrote more during my term as Vice Mayor and often articulated guidance such as the following. "Palo Alto must maintain this posture of dedication to open space to the greatest feasible extent for the benefit of present and future residence."

The following is something I wrote while on the City Council just to give you an idea of the issues with which I was dealing. "Palo Alto has a drug abuse problem. The ramifications of this problem are reflected in the high crime rate as well as the loss to society of the individuals directly involved. The goal must be measurable elimination of the problem, not maintenance of an ever-increasing burden. Housing for the elderly and low to moderate-income families has received much support in theory but little support in practice. To attain significant achievements in this area, we must reexamine the guidelines in view of funding source changes. Also, this must be done within the framework of good community understanding and acceptance. Responsive local transportation must be provided for the convenience of residents as well as for non-resident employees. A great portion of our traffic problem will be eliminated in so doing. There is a great need for Palo Alto and other communities to establish and work towards common objective particularly with regard to traffic transportation and land use." That is an example of the types of issues that were important to me at the time.

Some say I was a "militant moderate" while in office – I say I just wanted to do the right thing. An incident relating to a vote on a drug treatment facility resulted in me getting death threats by phone and briefly requiring around-the-clock security. I discussed the threats briefly with my wife, Virginia, but not with my sons. Virginia always thought it was best not to worry them. Neither of us took it very seriously until something happened at home a week later that made us realize things had changed for the Clay family.

One midweek night after I was appointed Vice Mayor of Palo Alto, Virginia and the boys heard some noises coming from the driveway area on the left side of our house. I was already asleep, as I had an early appointment with the Council the next morning. We had heard sounds at night before but not like these. They were not sounds of birds or small animals, nor were they from the swishing or rustling sounds of the branches and leaves in the trees outside on this breezy night. The sounds they were hearing were not familiar. One of the boys woke me out of my much-needed sleep and said a prowler was outside. I thought I was having a bad dream, but I wasn't, so with pajama bottoms on, I stepped into the slippers on the floor beside the bed and went to investigate. Since I had already received harmful threats, Virginia was sure that someone was outside intending to hurt us. Still, wishing this was all a nightmare, I could hear noise now, but it was coming from behind our house. We told the boys to stay in their rooms as Virginia and I hurried to the kitchen to call the police. She handed the receiver from the wall phone to me, while she dialed the rotary phone nervously. I couldn't help but notice Rodney tightly grabbing his baseball bat and holding it by his side as he stood in the doorway to his room.

At that moment, I realized I should have explained to the boys that there were threats sent to me because I was now the Vice Mayor. That thought quickly vanished, as I heard a voice on the line. It was the officer in charge at the local precinct. I said, "Hello this is Vice Mayor Roy Clay, and I want to report hearing suspicious noises outside my house - can you please send someone over to investigate in a hurry please." The officer responded, "Vice Mayor Clay are you located on Scripps Court?" I replied, "Yes officer." Then she said, "Don't worry. We sent a security detail over to your address this evening, and they reported their arrival outside your home about 20 minutes ago. That is likely what you hear. Were you not informed about these random around-the-clock security checks that will continue until the end of the year?" I told her I had been told about the extra security but was not sure when it would start. She radioed to the officers and asked them to ring the doorbell, introduce themselves and return to their curbside vehicle. She apologized for the confusion and alerted me to be aware of the security checks in the future. She also mentioned that she would advise any future officers to remain parked in their vehicles on future visits unless they notice something suspicious. I thanked her and went to the door to greet the officers. I reassured my family that everything was okay, put my arm around Rodney, and relieved him of that 34-inch Louisville Slugger he held tightly. We greeted the police officers together that night. Afterward, I had a discussion with my family about why we would have police protection going forward as long as I was in office as Vice Mayor. The boys took it well, and from that day on I committed myself to always be open with them about my work and about anything that may interfere with our family life. We all hugged and breathed a little easier afterward, and soon I was asleep again, resting my mind and body to step boldly into another relentless day at City Hall.

As much as I loved the business and political aspects of my life, I was just as happy spending time with my family. However, it was not as easy as before. Still, I managed to continue bowling nights with them, just less frequently. We also would shoot pool on our pool table at home two or three times a month. The boys were excellent players, but sometimes I think they would intentionally lose to me, just so they could hear me say, "Rack'em rackman," something I picked up from my pool hall days in Kinloch. I remember Virginia would laugh so much at how we carried on so much on those family nights. She laughed and cheered us on and always made sure we had plenty of snacks and drinks. She seemed to get a lot of joy from taking care of her guys. However, Roy, Jr took no pity on me as he was one of the best "pool sharks" in the Bay Area. He had already graduated from Cubberley High School and was on his way to the University of California - Santa Cruz, to study Physics. I was also attending soccer games that Chris was playing in, and I was coaching Rodney in baseball. I bought a catcher's mitt at Sears, and Rodney perfected his breaking pitches to me in the backyard. He could also "bring the heat" and within months, there were a few blisters on my catching hand courtesy of Rodney's high fastball.

We spent time doing activities with some of the other parents and their children, including Cliff Lamb, a local psychiatrist, and his wife Norma, and their three kids,

Michelle, Michael, and Skipper. Then there was Bill Green, an attorney, and his wife Loretta, who was originally a classical pianist, but she started a career in journalism and became a columnist for the Palo Alto Times, the San Jose Mercury, and other publications. We met them around 1970, and they had four kids, Billy, Roderick, Nicole, and Lisa.

I spent a lot of time serving others in the Palo Alto area, and I have no regrets, but my first priority was always my family. I was always there for my boys, and one incident comes to mind that is an example of that. My youngest son, Chris, played soccer for an American Youth Soccer Organization (AYSO) team, so always being supportive of their interests, I purchased a new soccer ball for him. He took the ball to soccer practice with him at a local field. The coach of his team, who happened to be a Palo Alto police officer, saw Chris leaving practice with his ball and assumed that Chris was trying to steal a team ball. Chris explained that it was his ball, but the coach did not believe him and took the ball from him. Chris came home so disappointed and told me what had happened. I was furious, especially since this coach knew that I was on the Palo Alto City Council at the time. Without hesitation, I called the coach and told him that the ball belonged to Chris, and I asked him to bring the ball back to us at the house and apologize to Chris for accusing him of stealing it. This would be one of several Palo Alto Police incidents that involved my sons and other talented and well-behaved children of color in the Palo Alto area. Incidents like this made me realize that all of our young people deserved better treatment from our city, and as an elected official, I was in a position to make a difference. There were many more goals to accomplish in Palo Alto. Equally as important, there was a much bigger business opportunity lurking. Was I up for the challenge?

Virginia and I representing the Palo Alto City Council at the 50 th Anniversary celebration of the long since closed Palo Alto Yacht Club

Photo with me and Virginia along with Roy Jr, Chris and Rodney for my Palo Alto City Council campaign promotional flyer

Cover of my Palo Alto City Council campaign promotional flyer

Me with my Roy L. Clay and Associates colleagues in our downtown
Palo Alto office

Chapter Eight

WHEN MY LIFE CHANGED
FOREVER

A tall, gray-haired clergyman leaned against the mahogany podium. In a slow, baritone-like voice, he said, "Emma Jean Clay was the salt of the earth," as he started the eulogy following a soloist's stirring soprano rendition of, "When you hear of my homegoing." I remember that day so well, as most of the family and friends who were present wiped their tear-filled eyes and some threw up their hands, waving them in response to the words of the Pastor of First Missionary Baptist Church in Kinloch. He was right about my mother, but I say she was that and a great deal more. Mother was the sugar and all the spices too. She was also my rock and my inspiration. It is often said that a philosopher is a person whose philosophical perspective makes meeting trouble with equanimity easier. That was my mother. She fit that description perfectly with her timeless words of wisdom. From the time I took my first breath, she never stopped wrapping her arms around me, influencing me to open my eyes to all dreams and possibilities, and shaping me into the audacious person I became. She was and still is my angel.

I received the inevitable call that my mother had passed away on October 4, 1976. I had just left a meeting about my plans to campaign for another term on the Palo Alto City Council, but politics was far from my mind after hearing the news about my mother, Emma Jean Clay. She had been suffering from Alzheimer's for a couple of years and was under the care of my sisters, Imogene and Hope, in Los Angeles. Because of this incurable illness, my mother, who had given birth to and raised nine children, lived her last days with little cognitive and physical abilities. Since our mother's passing, many of my siblings have died from Alzheimer's. I hope and pray a cure will be discovered soon for this disease that has devastated my family over the years.

Many friends and folks from the surrounding communities were at my mother's homegoing service, displaying respect for the woman who brought me into this world. Even the town pool hall owner, Deacon, was there. He is the same man who taught me how to run a business when I was a student. I noticed Deacon right away, and he saw me as well. He removed his fancy gold-banded, black-brimmed hat, something he rarely did. He wasn't much for words, but he did give me his signature wink, and I winked back. It was kind of his way of letting you know he cared. Lots of people back home just never felt comfortable at funerals, and that included old Deacon. Still, he made sure to pay his respects that day. I shook hands with and hugged many people who were there to honor my mother, but none of those hugs meant more than that wink from Deacon.

My beautiful, kind and loving mother, born just before the turn of the century on Thanksgiving Day in 1899, was no longer with us. Another chapter of my life was beginning, but I was ready. She had prepared me for it, and besides, I knew she would always be with me, smiling down and watching over me.

The Bicentennial year was almost over, and Jimmy Carter was about to be our new president. My mother had joined Daddy well before the winter weather settled in, though, no surprise to me. I know she was happy in paradise since she never liked snow and cold weather. She said it always made her bones ache.

I did not win my bid for reelection to the City Council in 1977, despite the campaigning efforts of my sons, my wife, and all my supporters who worked hard to try to keep me in office. It could have been because I was an independent thinking person. I was one who arrived at decisions through an objective review of both sides of issues and genuinely believed the city would be best served if each council member acted in this fashion, and to the contrary, I thought the city was ill-served by the block voting that was the norm in our city politics. I also tried to represent all segments of Palo Alto citizens, something that had not been done well before I took office. Also, my interest in housing and other social issues may have been too advanced for the majority of our citizens. Maybe I made some of the folks think too much, and I probably supported changes that were still uncomfortable for some people. I believe I was good for the city though. Sometimes it takes a person like me to get folks to start thinking differently, even if it's just one term. That's all the "stirring up" necessary to wake some people up. It's a long process, but I think I started the ball rolling in Palo Alto.

Sure, I was disappointed about not being reelected, but there is something to say about getting new blood into political offices more often. A person might work a little harder to get their priorities accomplished if they know they only had so much time to make it happen. Besides, elected officials can start feeling a little too powerful if they are in office too long. I almost did myself, even after only one term, but not as much as some of the others. I just knew that I had to come in and make some decisions early because I probably wouldn't get another crack at it. I did what my conscience told me to do while in office, and when it was time to move on, I did it with grace.

Before I left my political office, my life had already made an amazing turn for the better, so it made the bitter pill of losing the election easier to swallow. I had been successful in the "valley" before it was known as Silicon Valley. Therefore, I had the managerial skills and experience to do just about anything relating to computers, including running my own technology company. There were not too many people who knew the computer business as well as I did. So, with the field growing at such a fast pace, along with the vast network of technology professionals I had access to, I saw a golden opportunity to achieve my ultimate career goal of owning one of the premier technology companies in Silicon Valley. This venture would enable me to rise, metaphorically, from the "valley" to the "mountaintop" for much of the next two decades.

Tom Perkins' company, Kleiner Perkins, had been a client of my consulting firm, Roy Clay and Associates, for several years when I invited Tom for lunch at one of our favorite restaurants, about a mile from the Stanford campus in Palo Alto. My bold intention was to treat him to a good steak and then pitch an idea that I had for a new venture, one that would involve me acquiring a local electronics company that had been in existence since the 1970s. Since Tom was my friend, I was not as nervous about this meeting as most others would be, especially given Tom's penchant for unfiltered, often harsh feedback on new ideas. Still, I realized that it wasn't going to be easy by any stretch of the imagination. It would be important for me to keep my composure, be honest, and have a well-thought-out plan. I was mindful of that as I looked him directly in the eye and explained, in detail, how my company would manufacture and provide electrical safety test and measurement equipment. I did all this while trying to hold back the sweat from my brow.

Without hesitation, and after a perfect steak and glass of his favorite wine, Tom agreed to provide the venture capital to fund my startup. I was so happy that I almost jumped out of my seat, but I kept my cool and settled for pausing for a toast to the occasion with my friend, Tom. He also insisted on paying for the steaks that day, as he always did. ROD-L Electronics was on its way, with my unstoppable self leading the way. All the elements of success were there - confidence, desire, a passion for learning, and mutually respectful associations with good people like Tom Perkins.

I named the company ROD-L Electronics because that was the name my wife Virginia recommended. I was going to name the company after myself, (Roy L), but she thought it would be a great idea to name it after one of our boys, so we chose ROD-L, which was short for Rodney L, who was our middle son. In Virginia's words, "That name just had a special ring to it." Our company mission was to develop electrical testing technology that prevented any electrically operated device from posing a hazard, often lethal, to the user of that device, in the event of a power surge. The name of the test is dielectric withstand test, or High Potential (HiPot) test. Given the severity of safety, it was important to provide great products, so I immediately hired an amazing engineer from HP Labs to help me design one of our most successful products. From the beginning, ROD-L was insured by the highly regarded Chubb and Sons, which was a big selling point when promoting our products.

Operating as ROD-L Electronics (ROD-L), we developed the first electronically controlled Dielectric Withstand (HiPot) Tester. This was when the electronics industry was preparing for the impending 1980, Underwriters Laboratory (UL) requirement that mandated production-line hipot test. UL is America's leading authority on product safety certification, so this requirement was important and a great opportunity for our company. We (ROD-L) called upon industry leaders, AT&T Corporation, Hewlett-Packard Company, IBM Corporation, Tektronix Corporation, and Xerox Corporation, to partner with us to develop the specifications for the tester. The end result was that all external features, and some internal features of our ROD-L hipot testers, were specified by those previously mentioned partners. AT&T commissioned us (ROD-L) to implement the Federal Communications Commission's (FCC-Part 680) Hipot test requirement. IBM then refined our formula and commissioned us to develop several safety options.

Tektronix, Xerox, and Hewlett Packard gave us key feedback and helped us refine our products further. Ironically, even though Bill Hewlett and I didn't see eye to eye when I left HP, he ended up being a key contributor to our product features. Receiving and acting upon feedback from key customers is critical to the success of any business and certainly helped ROD-L develop a world-leading line of test equipment.

Each of our partners received and evaluated a production prototype article of the ROD-L hipot tester before it was released to the market. My team discovered that a product which previously passed the hipot test, may later fail, possibly due to shelf life. However, it is important to know that a manufacturer can significantly reduce its product legal liability exposure by producing a record that shows that a hipot test was made at the end of the assembly, even if an electrical insulation breakdown occurred later. At long last, my team and I had produced the first certified Underwriters Laboratory (UL) Listed Hipot and Ground Bond testers, and we decided that its product design would be of modular construct and upward compatible. We hoped that identifying and solving problems would be more straightforward. The quality of construction of the cabinets/package was particularly important to customers as well, and that design was modeled after the top-notch quality of HP's instruments. Lastly, we offered a five-year warranty on our products, which could be upgraded to a lifetime warranty. Demonstrating a commitment to product excellence was another key ingredient to the company's early success.

This was such an exciting time for me, as the technology was an instant success. It was quickly bought up by IBM, AT&T, and ironically my old company, HP. Sure, there were probably individuals who may have resented me having a viable business in the high-tech world of the valley. Still, at the end of the day, I deeply appreciated those businesses who supported and respected me for my company's excellent products and customer service. The support I received from HP was especially gratifying. My new company was technically one of the earliest portfolio companies of Kleiner and Perkins (KP), with Tandem being the largest. The venture capital giant would later go on to fund and incubate some of the world's largest technology companies.

I owed a great deal of my success to Tom Perkins, who always seemed to have my back. Still, much of my success with ROD-L Electronics was based on principles I learned and developed while working at HP, such as the following.

- Build high-quality products and charge a commensurate price.
- Treat all employees (from top to bottom) with respect.
- Recognize employee accomplishments and let them know their value to the company.
- Let employees know how their job "well done" leads to customer happiness and company success.

When I founded ROD-L Electronics, I had another vision in mind besides providing excellent products for my clients. It was also important to me to give back when it came to hiring practices. So, I made it a point to hire people of all races and nationalities from a local job training program, named Opportunities Industrial Center - West (OICW). I connected with Reverend Leon Sullivan, who founded the first Opportunities Industrial Center (OIC) in the mid-1960s in Philadelphia, Pennsylvania. He brought the program out west to East Palo Alto and created (OICW) with support from other local leaders and the support and leadership of David Packard (of HP). David Packard's support was driven by a desire to create opportunities for the lower-income area of East Palo Alto, and to help expand HP's pool of available talent. This is also documented in the book, The *HP Way*. We also continued to recruit from Historically Black Colleges, and we hired some minority students from nearby Stanford University.

The company did well as the sale of computers, especially the Intel microprocessors, had skyrocketed in the late 1970s and into the early 1980s. Tom Perkins' Tandem Computer Company was soaring as well. It seemed that everything he tried in business turned into gold. He was a man who, by his own description, was tall, lean, and impatient. Others say he could create tension in a room simply by walking in. I would agree somewhat, but I found him to be a man who simply knew what he wanted and knew how to get it – which mainly consisted of knowing who he could depend on and building strong relationships with them. To my good fortune, I happened to be one of those people.

In 1982, Roy, Jr was in graduate school at Boston University, pursuing a master's degree in electrical engineering on a full scholarship. He had earned a degree in physics from the University of California - Santa Cruz, which was close by, so he assisted me at ROD-L during summer and holiday breaks. He continued to work with me at ROD-L for a few months, but his goal was to get a graduate degree. He wanted to go east for graduate school, and he decided to go just about as far east as possible. I missed his help at ROD-L, and Virginia and I just missed him being around.

My sons all had roles in the development of ROD-L. Roy, Jr worked with me before he left for graduate school. My youngest son, Chris, worked with us during the summers while attending UC Berkeley. He graduated in 1987 with a degree in electrical engineering and worked full-time with the company as a product design engineer. He designed a few new pieces of test equipment while he was at ROD-L, then he took two years off from 1989 to 91 to pursue an MBA at UCLA. After graduating from UCLA business school, he returned to work with us at ROD-L.

Rodney also worked with us while finishing school and after graduation from San Jose State University. Rodney worked with us part-time while he was a student at San Jose State University. He began by assembling mechanical parts, a function of the product production process. After he graduated with his degree in marketing, he took on a role on the marketing side of the company. He was responsible for buying ads in trade journals and scheduling and coordinating our participation in trade shows and other marketing-related activities. It was his niche at the time, and he performed exceptionally well.

Chris and Rodney were also learning the game of golf by caddying for me when I played leisurely. Roy, Jr was a great pool player. He played off and on throughout the next few decades, winning minor tournaments and even filling in occasionally as a house pro in a large San Jose pool hall about twenty years ago. That was when he was invited to audition in Hollywood for a sports commercial - as a pool player, of course!

You could say that passing on the importance of education to my sons was a commitment that I made, just as my parents passed along the value of education to me. It certainly paid off because not only did they become well educated, but it was a good way to create my own little workforce since all three of them worked at ROD-L for a good part of their careers. Some may cry nepotism, but I'd say that's one impressively good way to fill vacancies. What was good for the business also helped in building our close-knit family. My sons and I worked together, played together, and there were the occasional family and work spats as well, but we never let anything come between us. That's another value that was passed along from my Kinloch days, and it's amazing how our family is still so close and supportive of each other today.

Since the business was doing so well, I would often treat myself to a round of golf early in the morning before starting work. I began playing golf while working at HP and absolutely loved the game. I think the combination of it challenging you physically, as well as being a thinking man's game, drew me in. However, it was not easy for me to meet other golfers in those times, since most of them were white and were not so likely to include me in their foursomes back in the sixties and early seventies.

I'm sure I became a familiar face at some of the area courses, although it took them a while to realize I wasn't there to caddy. It was not much fun playing alone, so I always talked some of my black professional friends into hitting the links with me. I always hoped their wives did not blame me for their golf habits, but I'm fairly sure they did. We became regulars at the golf course, like a black golfing club. They were doctors, lawyers, engineers, mathematicians, all professional men. Friends like Bill Green, Jim Denton, Dave Jordan, John Minor, Cliff Lamb, Ed Williams, Bill McCullough, Jim Lockhart, Miles McAfee, Harold Boyd, and a few others, would join me from time to time. It even got to the point where the white golfers were no longer asking us how to purchase golf balls or rent a golf cart. Those were the days.

There was also a fantastic club for black golfers that we all belonged to that was named the Spear Golf Club. The club was started to promote organized golfing for the enjoyment of its members and guests. It is great to see that there are many women who are members and compete now as well. In the early 1970's the club became affiliated with the Western State Golf Association (WSGA), whose goal is to promote organized golf throughout the states of Arizona, California, Colorado, Nevada, Oregon, and Washington. Over twenty golf clubs are now members of WSGA, including Spear Golf Club. The club still hosts an annual tournament each year, and a portion of the proceeds benefits Junior Golf programs.

Bill Green, my good friend and a member of our golfing group, had a son, Billy (Bill, Jr), who was an excellent track athlete at the time. Bill, an attorney, had been an outstanding college athlete himself. Bill Jr had broken records throughout high school. With an outstanding performance at the 1980 Olympic Trials, he made the 1980 US Olympic Team. Tragically, he never had the chance to compete, as that was the year the US boycotted the Olympics. It all went down on President Jimmy Carter's watch. Iranian militants stormed the U.S. Embassy in Tehran and took some Americans hostage. To make matters more tense, just about a month later, the Soviet Union executed an invasion of Afghanistan. It seems that the only luck in America at this time was bad luck.

Just imagine the shock and disappointment it was to Bill and his family. They had planned to travel to the Olympics that year, but they seemed to handle that situation as well as they possibly could. Bill, an attorney, and his wife Loretta, a journalist, just seemed to always have the right words to say while expressing their disappointment to their friends and neighbors. I don't think I could have handled it so well. All of our golfing families felt bad for Bill, Jr, during this time in our history, which included more disappointments ahead for America.

It had been a difficult first few years for the Carter Administration, and there were more bad breaks to come. A series of domestic economic problems were ahead, including mass increases in gasoline prices, rising inflation, and high unemployment that were also coming to the forefront. Americans had already been asked from the beginning of Carter's term to conserve energy, as he donned sweaters and reduced his usage of gas and electricity, as an example. He continued to ask businesses and consumers to cut back on energy as well. Since Americans were used to the good life and a relatively strong economy, this plan did not work well. However, in Silicon Valley, business was going well. The valley had emerged as the world's leader in developing silicon-based integrated circuits, the microprocessor, as well as the microcomputer, among other technologies. That is why the aforementioned problems like inflation, gasoline shortages, and cutbacks throughout the rest of the nation were a stark contrast to the success we were having in Silicon Valley.

President Carter was a good man in so many ways, but he lost his reelect bid the following year. Soon there was a new "leading man" in the White House. Former Hollywood actor and California Governor, Ronald Reagan, was now our president.

President Reagan effectively got the economy back on track as things seemed to take a turn for the better around the country. I was running a vital company, my sons were coming into their own, and I was playing golf more regularly again. Things just seemed to be headed in the right direction.

Then came the end of October 1982, and with it came some devastating news to our family. We were nearing the holiday season, a time for parties and good cheer, but my wife Virginia, who I always considered the strongest of anyone I had ever known, had not been feeling well. We both had noticed a lump on one of her breasts. She told me she was afraid to get it checked out, but we had no choice. I told her that she would not be alone, and so the next day I drove her to the hospital for a diagnosis. I was shaking so much that it affected my driving. After a few miles on the road, I just put two hands on the steering wheel and fixed my eyes directly on the road for the remainder of the twenty-minute drive. I wanted to glance over at her and say something sweet, but I just couldn't do it without getting too emotional.

When we arrived at the hospital, it did not feel real. I knew I had to be strong for her but walking through those emergency room doors was never something I felt comfortable with, and this time was the most difficult of all. I squeezed her hand, and she moved closer to me as we checked in. It was the typical busy, frantic look of an ER, so that seemed to be the only thing normal that morning. It would be a slow wait for me over the next two hours after she was whisked away by a fast-paced, prematurely gray-haired woman, who appeared to be only slightly older than Virginia. I thought to myself, *my hair would be gray, too, if I were around so much pain and sickness every day.*

After they finished the examination, Virginia and I walked out of that place, hoping for the best, but understanding that the worst could be overwhelming. There was so much silence at home over the next nerve-racking days as we awaited the results. Every time the phone rang, my heart fluttered. Then the dreaded call came early one morning; Virginia had cancer. That was the day that changed my life forever. I knew the challenges ahead would be the most difficult I had ever faced. I consoled my wife as much as I could, and we prepared ourselves for what was next.

It was two days later that I anxiously drove Virginia to the Palo Alto Medical Clinic to see Dr. Bob Jamplis, the Executive Director. The results of the diagnosis had already been sent to him, and he immediately suggested chemotherapy and scheduled surgery for her as well. Dr. Jamplis, who I knew from my work on the City Council, and while on the Palo Alto Medical Foundation board, was great with Virginia, and his advice to me was also needed. Initially, I said to myself, *"How could this have happened to me. After all, I am the founder of a successful Silicon Valley Company?"* Dr. Jamplis must have been reading my mind when he placed his hand on my shoulder, looked me in the eye, and suggested that I seek counseling while Virginia was going through her difficult chemo sessions and the mastectomy surgery. He said that he recommended it for husbands who had to watch their wives fight this disease.

After several counseling sessions, I realized that I had been feeling sorry for myself. It was Virginia who needed empathy. Though she seemed more than ready to fight the pain and hardship she was facing, she would need my love, care, and strength to support her now. I drove her to every doctor's appointment, and we began to have some very deep and personal chats together at night, which made me realize she was stronger than I had ever thought before. She told me that she did not want any sympathy from friends and that she wanted her illness to be our private concern. During her illness, I observed her calling friends who were ill, showing her concern for their wellbeing.

This was when I had to be there in every way imaginable for Virginia. Even my business had to take a back seat, so thank goodness I had some more than capable staff to manage things at ROD-L for me. Still, there were days when my employees would shed tears after almost every staff meeting when I met with them. After Dr. Jamplis performed Virginia's surgery, I am certain I looked as tired my team as I felt during that period when my sons and I waited on Virginia hand and foot. Virginia's sister Joyce, who was still in the area, came to visit as often as she could and would bring her daughter Lori, who we called Joyce's "mini-me," along with her. She and Virginia also talked by phone almost every day, as I recall. It all reminded me of when I was injured playing football as a child and how everyone took care of me after I had surgery. However, what Virginia was going through was much more serious. She was fighting for her life, and I had a new admiration for her. Our home, which had always been full of cheer and bustling with activity, was quiet most days and nights, and our hearts were heavy. Between the boys and I, we gave all that we could to comfort her.

Fortunately, my friend Tom Perkins came through for us again. One of the companies that Tom started was Genentech, which was and still is a biotechnology company dedicated to pursuing groundbreaking science to discover and develop medicines for people with serious and life-threatening illnesses. They had developed medicines for cancer treatment patients, and Tom made sure Virginia was well taken care of as if she was family. They also offered some experimental drugs to her, but Dr. Jamplis rejected that, and we agreed with him. Between Genentech, and the advice of the good people at the Palo Alto Medical Foundation, whose board I had served on, my wife had the best care possible. That was a blessing for our family. She also committed to healthy living, regarding appropriate diet, exercise, and rest, a decision that also likely extended her life by several years. After a year or so, Virginia began to feel better and went into remission for several years.

We gradually resumed some of the good things in life that we had previously enjoyed. We went out for dinner and entertainment more regularly, and she joined me on some of my business trips. Sometimes, our sons, Rodney and Chris, who were still at home, traveled with us too. I later found out that Virginia had talked to the boys and advised them about helping me with her, and about helping with the business. She was always an advocate of keeping the family together and supporting one another.

Those were some interesting times. The record-setting album, *Thriller,* was released, and it became a big hit around 1983. It wasn't quite our style, but Chris and Rodney seemed to enjoy it, along with some of the other music of that time. We got a kick out of watching Chris and Rodney try to match Michael Jackson's moves when they were at home on weekends. All I can say is that MJ didn't have to worry about competition from our boys, or anybody else for that matter. Virginia had started to read more. I recall her reading, *The Color Purple* by Alice Walker, who won the Pulitzer Prize for fiction for that work in April of 1983. This was a period in our history when CDs, the Internet, and the first camcorders were introduced to the world. Microsoft Word was first released during this time, but the version designed for the windows operating system was not released until 1989. The most meaningful thing that happened was when the Dr. Martin Luther King national holiday was declared by President Reagan in November of 1983, and although the first celebration was not until 1986, it was worth the wait.

In the spring of 1984, the entire computer industry went into a downturn, and Tandem's earnings fell 80 percent. That called for tightening its internal controls and refocusing attention on a stronger, more centralized management. They rebounded and became the dominant manufacturer of fault-tolerant computer systems for ATM networks, banks, stock exchanges, telephone switching centers, and other similar commercial transaction processing applications, requiring maximum uptime and zero data loss. I was incredibly happy that things worked out because a strong computer industry was good for ROD-L Electronics. They (Tandem) remained independent until 1997, when they were acquired by Compaq Computers. Compaq was later acquired by HP.

By the mid-eighties, Virginia was becoming more active, volunteering in the community whenever she had the time. One group that she became a founder of was the Girl's Club of the Mid-Peninsula in East Palo Alto, and as if I weren't busy enough, she asked me to serve as president of the organization. Well, I never could say no to Virginia, so there I was with another important commitment to the community, but this time it was to East Palo Alto, on the other side of the freeway, where I was needed more. That city did not have the money and resources like Palo Alto.

I still managed to play golf regularly with my friends, and with the black golfer's group, one of many groups throughout the country that were necessary because of the ugly biases that we faced back then. Somehow, we never seemed to be bitter and never let it get us down, always hoping that the days ahead would be better. Our group of fantastic golfers was together almost every Saturday, playing golf, making wagers, laughing it up, and more importantly, doing some brotherly bonding. Still, I kept thinking that something big was about to take place, soon, involving me again, but what would it be?

Chapter Nine

THEY COULDN'T STOP ME!

I started playing golf in the 1960s, not realizing the impact the game would have on my life. With the help of my early "Flex Time" concept that I designed initially for my staff at HP, I would start my workday late and finish late, so there were times when I played nine holes before work. I was on the links two or three weekdays a week. Sometimes, I played with a couple of my employees before an important business meeting. After those games, our meetings tended to be livelier and more upbeat. I continued that management philosophy after starting my own company, and it was always an excellent way to build a family culture within the organization. By the mid-1980s, I had played golf for twenty years, and my intrigue with the game was only topped by my love and devotion to my wife and sons. Despite all the time I spent on the fairways and running ROD-L Electronics, I was still committed to spending time with my family at home.

Virginia and I were now closer than ever, and because of my business success, I was able to provide her with anything she desired. More importantly, as an entrepreneur, I could choose how much time I spent at the office. On a cold January afternoon, I decided to leave the office early and watch the Space Shuttle lift off with Virginia. We were so excited for the young astronauts and their families. Sadly, disaster struck right before our eyes. Emotions went from optimism to sorrow moments after liftoff when the Space Shuttle Challenger broke apart 73 seconds into its flight, killing all seven crew members aboard. It was the first fatal accident involving an American spacecraft in flight. We wept thinking about how the families of the crew members would be affected after this tragedy, specifically Ron McNair and Christa McAuliffe. Ron McNair was on his second mission after becoming the second black astronaut to fly to space two years earlier. Another person aboard, whom we admired, was Christa McAuliffe. She was a teacher from Maryland who was to be the first educator in space under NASA's Teacher in Space project. Both were HBCU graduates, and at the time of the tragedy, both were married with two young children. Incidents, like the Space Shuttle disaster, make you realize how special it is to be alive. Virginia and I vowed to live every day to the fullest after that disaster.

That same year, I was introduced to a member of the famed San Francisco Olympic Club when he visited the Palo Alto Municipal Golf Course. From that moment on, I was never the same. I had always heard so much about that club, and there was no doubt about it; the history was legendary. Perhaps the most noteworthy fact about the club, to me, was that it did not admit blacks to its membership. I had never given any thought to visiting the place, until Roger Staples and I started a conversation about golf. Once he realized my passion for the game, he invited me to apply for membership and pledged that he would support me through the process. Yes, good old Roger opened up that can of worms. He explained what I would have to do to get things started. I thought to myself, *this is one crazy white guy to assume that a black man's application would be considered by the club. He had me wondering, what if I am admitted?* You see, I remembered that Roger had just served as President of the Olympic Club in 1985, so he must have known that this was the time for the club to catch up with the times and include minorities and women.

The prestigious Olympic Club was founded on May 6, 1860, by 23 charter members. History has it that they turned their informal gymnastics training sessions, held in the backyard of gold rush artists, Arthur and Charles Christian Nahl, into a lasting institution. It is the oldest Athletic Club in the United States. In the 1800s alone, the membership roster included names like Mark Twain, William Randolph Hearst, Charles Crocker, Leland Stanford, James G. Fair, and John Mackey. Athletes such as "Gentleman Jim" Corbett, winner of the World heavyweight title in 1892, also belonged to the Olympic Club. Pioneering Olympic Club champions include swimmer, J. Scott Leary, the first American to swim 100 yards in 60 seconds, and shot putter, Ralph Rose, who won six Olympic medals and held seven national AAU titles.

The Olympic Club sent 23 athletes to the 1924 Olympic Games in Paris. That was the largest delegation from a single club.

Football was also king during the 1920s, and the club celebrated undefeated seasons in 1925 and 1928. Even with schedules pitting the club against local college teams, the club was formidable, at least against the white-only competition. The club's first permanent clubhouse, downtown on Post Street, opened in 1893. Unfortunately, it was destroyed in the Great 1906 earthquake and fire. During this dark hour, Club President, William F Humphrey, emerged as the driving force of the institution. He led the Olympic Club for almost a half-century. Olympic rebuilt its clubhouse on Post Street and reopened in 1912. In 1918, the Olympic Club assumed operations of the financially distressed Lakeside Golf Club, therefore gaining a country home. By 1922, the club had purchased enough acreage to replace the original golf course with two 18-hole golf courses as well. The club added a tennis complex in 1936.

In 1955, the club hosted its first U.S. Open. I didn't follow golf much in the 1950s, but after doing a little research, I learned that Jack Fleck, an unknown from Iowa, birdied two of the last four holes of the final round to force a playoff with Ben Hogan. Fleck won that first Open at Olympic, and the Lake Course established its reputation as a host to upsets. Billy Casper overcame Arnold Palmer in 1966, which I remember so well. Scott Simpson edged Tom Watson in 1987. And later on, Lee Jansen defeated Payne Stewart in

1998. During the 2012 U.S. Open, Webb Simpson emerged from four shots back to take the title. The club, with its three golf courses, remains much more than just a Country Club in a glowing variety of ways. Throughout its storied history, one tarnished distinction about this otherwise prominent West Coast landmark lingered on shamefully even through the civil rights movement and beyond. Racism and exclusionary policies still existed at the time of my introduction to the club.

The meticulously landscaped Lake Course property had a few magnificent views of the Golden Gate Bridge. However, it was still restricting blacks from its distinguished membership, and now it was under pressure to admit minorities and women. At a time when race and color in America should not have been significant in our lives, people like me were still not enjoying equal rights in our nation.

After all I had overcome and accomplished, I still found myself wondering if I would be accepted into a country club in San Francisco, a progressive, integrated city, that included people from a multiplicity of ethnic backgrounds. Remember, we were not in the deep South, such as where the Augusta (GA) National Country Club was still operating under exclusionary practices. In 1975, Lee Elder was the first black golfer allowed to play in The Masters Tournament, the Professional Golfer's Association's (PGA) iconic major event held annually at the esteemed Augusta National in Augusta, Georgia. However, the club did not lift its white-only restrictions for membership until 1990. It would be twenty-two years later, in the summer of 2012, before Augusta National invited former U.S. Secretary of State, Condoleezza Rice, and South Carolina financier, Darla Moore to become the club's first female members.

I remembered the day that Elder stepped onto the first hole at Augusta National, as my golfing partners and I welled up with tears after he teed up and hit his first drive. It meant so much to us then, but now here I was, years later, still hesitant about applying for membership to the Olympic Club. As always, my wife pushed me to apply and become their first black member. Sometimes I think she felt I was put here on earth to make "good trouble" and change the world, but honestly, I was no John Lewis. I just wanted to play golf, not be a martyr for the movement, but to play the best course possible, just like any other golf-loving guy.

My company, ROD-L Electronics, was growing fast, and we had a good staff to manage the day-to-day operations, so I had the time and resources to join the Olympic Club. At the time, my sons were around to help out as well. Chris had just finished college at UC Berkeley, Roy Jr had recently moved back to the East Coast, and Rodney was working part-time at the company while finishing his bachelor's degree at San Jose State University.

When I was informed that a San Francisco city attorney had filed suit against the club, demanding it begin admitting women and minorities or lose its lease on the land where the golf courses and other sports facilities were built,

I decided to go for it. That and the fact that the club's former president was recommending me had me extremely confident about being admitted. I also wanted to play that historic golf course at Olympic, so why not? It was just me doing what I do best, challenging myself to accomplish the seemingly impossible.

The wait after submitting my formal application was excruciating with each day and restless night that went by. Then finally, I got word - I was in! I became the first black man admitted to the club, followed by printing executive, Jessie Knight, who was not a golfer and came in initially as a social member. After I was admitted, an article was printed in the SF Examiner announcing that the Olympic Club had admitted its first black members. Here I was being *"the first"* again and making history, which seemed to be the story of my life. Still, I was also excited about joining the club for personal reasons. I received so many congratulatory phone calls that I just couldn't answer them all. I told my sons that I could not wait to get out on that golf course as an official member.

Then in the evening after the article was published, I came home to find, as usual, the answering machine blinking with a new voicemail alert. I clicked play and couldn't believe what I heard. "N____, you better not show your black face at the Olympic Club, or you and your entire family are dead!!!" I played it over and realized that this was not a prank from the tone and anger of the voice on the other line. My heart started racing uncontrollably. I was sweating, and my fingers were trembling. The possibility of someone hurting my family had me feeling scared, vulnerable, and angry. *What should I do now?* That was one of the many thoughts on my mind, as I attempted to calm myself, breathing slowly and deeply. As a former Palo Alto Vice Mayor, I was able to secure around-the-clock security and surveillance for my family and our home in Palo Alto, so here we were again, needing 24-hour security because of racially driven threats to my family and me. It was hard to imagine this in 1987 in Northern California. Just think. This was not the 1950s deep South!! This was the same year that President Reagan made the "Tear down that wall" speech, referring to the Berlin Wall, but we were having trouble just admitting a black man to a country club without hate and resistance in what we thought was a progressive city.

After receiving the death threat, I seriously considered withdrawing from the club's membership. This was one time in my life when I was feeling defeated and not strong enough to stay the course. I had faced so much racism in my life, and I suppose it may have been finally wearing me down. I gave it some thought but did not want to put my family in any kind of danger. When I told Virginia I would not accept the membership, she stopped in her tracks, turned around, and in her unmistakable voice of anger and frustration, said, "Wasn't Jackie Robinson your hero? Did he walk away from the Dodgers?" Then she continued to put some dishes away in the kitchen. That hit home with me, and she knew it would. I also thought about how strong she was during her battle with cancer, which put a new perspective on what I was dealing with. There was silence, then I walked towards her, reached for her hand, hugged her, and thanked her for that little reminder of what "number 42" did at a much higher level. I also thanked her for always showing me what it means to be tough when adversity rears its head. She made me realize that if Jackie Robinson could do it in the Big Leagues with the world watching, then I certainly could do it at that country club. Virginia was always that angel, pushing me to be relentless in the pursuit of my goals, and forever nudging me never to be afraid to step outside of my comfort zone.

That always seemed to happen. Either my wife or my mother would always be there, like angels on my shoulders, always pushing me, giving me confidence, and reminding me not to use racism or any other setback as an excuse not to win. Just a little push is all I needed, so I faced the music and the heat in Virginia's kitchen that night, if you will, as she always knew that there were not too many kitchens whose heat I couldn't stand. So, I accepted the membership to the Olympic Club and never looked back. It wasn't easy, but I did it. I hoped that the club's old-timers would become comfortable with seeing me there, and not mistake me for a caddy or the shoeshine guy. I was convinced that once they got to know me, they would realize that I just wanted the same things in life that they did, and in this case, that translated to getting a chance to play some good golf on the famous Lake golf course at the Olympic Club. That was the happiness I wanted to pursue. Was that asking too much?

Situations like this always made life so much more complicated for black men and women in those days and even now, which could be a factor in why we tend to have more stress-related illnesses. Author James Baldwin wrote, "To be black and conscious in America is to be in a constant state of rage." I never felt the pain Baldwin experienced; he left the country he loved to escape threats and harassment for simply asking our lawmakers and leaders to do better in providing equality for all Americans, instead of just the privileged who were usually white. Looking back at all the challenges I had faced - segregated schools, police brutality and harassment, job discrimination, housing discrimination, death threats, and more, I certainly understood Baldwin's words. His statement was simply a cry for all those who did not have a voice, in hopes of making our nation stand up to its original promise of liberty and justice for all. I still say today that my wife was the one who helped me remain levelheaded through my many years of experiencing unfair treatment because of my race. It's too bad Mr. Baldwin didn't have someone in his corner as I did. I didn't have to go so far to feel safe, comfortable, and confident. I was fortunate to have Virginia beside me every difficult step of the way.

The first time I played golf at the club after becoming a club member, I was very nervous as I approached the tee at the first hole on the Lake course; it was one of three golf courses on the Olympic property. I didn't sleep much the night before, but I didn't feel tired. An extremely large window overlooked the first tee from the pro shop, so I sensed that many members, caddies, and staff were watching. That newspaper article about me breaking the color line, and the death threat had drawn much attention, but I didn't turn around to see who was there. So much was going through my mind. I was reflecting on the heroic moments of Jackie Robinson and Lee Elder, and thinking about my Kinloch roots, my family, and the legacy I was passing on to them. I wanted to play well and not embarrass myself since many assumed that being black, I would not be very good.

I had become an expert at being the "first black," so I realized as soon as I laced up my golf shoes that I was representing people of color that day. More than anything, I wanted to be remembered not just for being the first, but for being a darn good golfer. The other three guys in the foursome went before me, so now it was my turn. Their tee shots were ok but not great, so that took some pressure off of me. I had already told them I had not played in a while, so I felt better playing last. *Just a little sandbagging won't hurt anybody,* I thought. Besides, I had waited a long time for this moment, so I played it up.

My journey into the club started with a solid par on the first hole! You would have thought it was the U.S. Open, which had already been held at the Olympic Club earlier that year. I stayed focused on the tee, the ball, and that impeccable tree-lined fairway, and then I pinched myself to make sure I wasn't dreaming. I stepped into the tee box, teed it up, took one deep breath, and hit my normal low draw right down the middle.

I don't think I breathed out until the ball stopped rolling in the middle of the fairway. I remember hearing applause, confirming that I had an audience, and then I heard "great shot" yelled out behind me as I impulsively raised my fist in the air. My three partners' mouths dropped almost in unison. The oldest of the three said, "Welcome to Olympic, young man." Another said, after a pat on my back, "I thought you hadn't played in a while. I can't wait to see what you do when you play regularly." I responded humbly, "It was just beginner's luck."

When we got to the green, I two-putted for a solid par on the first hole. I should have birdied the hole after that excellent shot off the tee, but after blowing the first put, I figured a par was a good way to start, and I didn't want to show off too much on my first day. I played well that cool, breezy day, finishing with the second-best score. In the coming months, I continued to improve as I learned the course and the weather got warmer. I have told this story of my first time playing at the Olympic Club many times, and somehow the details always seem to change as I get older, but one or two things stay the same. I proved that I did not get into the club because I was black. I was admitted because I belonged. I became the first African American to play that course as a full golf member, on the manicured fairways of the Olympic Club in its 130-year history.

After the initial cold shoulders and lukewarm reception when I joined the Olympic Club, I quickly engaged myself in club activities and became close friends with a surprisingly large number of the club members. I was a single-digit handicap golfer, which was just as good as most and better than many of the members, and I continued at that level well into my mid to late sixties. It was my dream not only to play golf at the Olympic, but to be one of the better players there, and I did just that. There were those members who were still unenthusiastic, at best, about me being there, but I had also made many good friends in a surprisingly short amount of time.

One of the benefits of being a member of the club was that I had reciprocal visitation to other championship courses, enabling me to travel around the country, with my family joining me. I was able to play championship courses like Winged Foot Country Club in West Chester County, New York, Medina Country Club in Medina County, Ohio, and other amazing clubs across the country. These trips were fun little getaways, and there were activities and amenities at each of the properties for all of us to enjoy. Chris, Rodney, and I were the golf lovers, so you could always find us on the golf course, working on our games. Virginia enjoyed the spa facilities, or just relaxing by the pool with a good book. Once, Roy Jr was with us, and he was the talk of the table tennis and pool table room. He brought his talents to the country clubs only a couple of times, but when he did, people would gather around in awe as they watched him dominate everyone brave enough to challenge him. As far as I know, he's still the undisputed country club champion.

Soon, things were not going so well for my wife. I first noticed it after returning home from a couple of those weekend trips visiting other country clubs. She had begun to drink heavily, mostly when we were home, but she would also have an extra cocktail when we were out for dinner or at social events. This is something I had never noticed before. Then there were times when she was a little cranky, and she said the drinking helped calm her down. My sons noticed it as well and questioned me about it. I hoped it was just a phase of some kind and that it would eventually go away.

Virginia eventually revealed to me that there was a reason for her unusual and uncharacteristic behavior. She had come out of her remission, as the cancer that had struck her earlier in the 1980s, had returned. She was afraid that she would not make it this time based on the doctor's prognosis. It hurt my heart to think she would have to battle this illness again. I was initially confused because I thought she would want me to stay home more and not make so many visits to the Olympic Club. However, she surprised me by saying she wanted me to continue playing golf and continue with my same business obligations. I continued to play golf, but one of the benefits of being a member of the Olympic club was that I was able to spend lots of quality time with my family there. One of our favorite and most memorable occasions there was the club's Mother's Day brunch we attended, with Virginia being the queen of the day.

She also told me and the boys that after she completed her chemotherapy, she wanted to travel again and continue living a full and active life. That is why I think it is important to ask a loved one, battling an illness like cancer, to let you know what they want from you, instead of you telling them what you think is important. She wanted us all to live more than ever before, and it turned out to be a good way to manage our crisis. We all pitched in to assist Virginia. Her sister, who had moved further north, started to visit more frequently. Chemotherapy would be scheduled soon, and Virginia seemed to be handling it like a trooper.

The doctor informed us that the cancer was spreading to her bones, which was causing a lot of pain. After Virginia started the chemo treatments, she quickly lost her hair in patches, but from what I recall, she was never fully bald. She didn't complain either. She just wore a scarf on her head until her hair grew back. She slowly lost weight, over time, as well. That was another effect of the treatments and the cancer itself.

The Bay Area Earthquake struck on October 17, 1989, less than two months before the Cold War officially ended. It was an interesting time in our history, especially for our community and my family. Virginia was at home watching the almost crosstown World Series between both our area home teams, the Oakland A's and San Francisco Giants. I was at the Olympic Club wrapping up a round of golf, before heading home to watch the rest of the game. When the earthquake hit, it startled Virginia so much that she recalled standing in a doorway and holding on for dear life. With many roads closed, my drive back home from San Francisco, which usually took forty minutes, lasted nearly four hours. The anxiety was building with each minute for Virginia, as she waited anxiously for me to arrive safely. Taking deep breaths often to calm her nerves, she was worried that because of the possible destruction, she may never see me again and feared that she could be left widowed and battling cancer on her own. Needless to say, I arrived home safely. We hugged, then we checked to make sure our family members were safe. Baseball and the World Series were far from our minds the rest of that night.

I was still very active at the Olympic Club and running my very successful business, with plenty of help from my sons and some outstanding employees. Sometimes I wonder how I found the energy, but I was always there like clockwork. I just kept ticking, working and playing hard, while also caring for my lovely Virginia above all. A few years after joining the club, I was so well respected, that I was voted onto the board of directors and eventually became president of the golf club. That did not seem possible when I was on the outside looking in, but it was another example of people giving each other a chance. Once you get past differences in appearance and commit to knowing a person, you either like him or her, or you don't. You find that we are strikingly similar, with indistinguishable needs and values, wanting the same things for our families and children.

Just when I thought I had been fully accepted into this club, a strange thing happened. After being elected to the club's board of directors, my picture was placed on the clubhouse wall along with the other directors, something that had been practiced for decades. A few days later, someone anonymously removed my picture overnight. It opened a lot of the members' eyes as to what I faced every day because of my race, no matter what position or title I held or ascended to. Many of them said they had never experienced anything like that before. One of my staunch supporters at the club, who was Caucasian, stood up for me and removed every other picture from the wall. He said, "If Roy's picture is going to be removed, then all the others must come down!" It was sort of like the iconic scene in Spike Lee's movie, *Do The Right Thing*, when one of the characters asked the Sal's Pizzeria owner, "Why are there no brothers on the wall?" while pointing in the direction of dozens of pictures of only white celebrities lining the walls of the seating area of the fictional pizzeria that was located in an overwhelmingly black neighborhood in Brooklyn, NY. In my situation, there were no revolts by the patrons as in Lee's film, but there certainly were many members who stood by me and made it apparent that I was as important as any other member of the club. Their support made me realize that I had made the right choice by accepting the Olympic Club membership just a few years earlier.

The summer of 1991 brought about one of my fondest memories. We traveled, as a family, to Asia for three weeks while doing business and giving Virginia a chance to see more of the world. My niece, Denise, also joined us on this trip. It was an unforgettable experience for everyone as we flew from San Francisco and spent time in Malaysia, Singapore, and Hong Kong. Denise is my brother Charles' daughter and is sort of the daughter I never had. She was also always like a sister to my boys. So naturally, we enjoyed it when she visited and traveled with us. She says that trip to Asia was one of the most memorable moments of her life.

Denise still talks about being amazed at how much energy I had on that trip. At a recent family virtual meeting, we discussed some of our travels, and she said, "Uncle Roy never stopped on that trip." She went on to explain as if it was yesterday, "He worked and played hard, and whatever there was to explore in those Asian cities, we did it. My cousins and I were so tired at the end of each day, but not him. We would be the last diners in the restaurant, and he'd begin talking about our next day's adventures." Then Roy, Jr followed her words. "Yes. Mom would say, 'Sometimes your father just doesn't have any going home sense when he's out having a good time.'" Now that I think of it, I was like that from time to time. That's the part of me that keeps me driven, I guess, always wanting and reaching for more. We didn't rest for long after that trip.

Soon after, Virginia and I spent three weeks in Europe with my youngest son, Chris, and the following summer, we traveled to Europe for three weeks with Rodney and Chris. The traveling did not stop there. We also revisited some of our favorite country clubs around America, making stops in New York, Florida, and Ohio. It was amazing playing golf at some of the best clubs in the country, including Winged Foot, Medina, and West Chester Country Club again, and also Lake Nona (Florida) for the first time. This was one way to keep Virginia active and enjoy life together as a family. She smiled a lot during those trips, and we smiled back at her. It was cathartic for us all. We were truly a team.

In 1992, I was instrumental in forming the Winged O Foundation at the club (now The Olympic Club Foundation). The Olympic Club Foundation's byline today is "Giving Wings to Youth." My intention, in the beginning, was that most of the foundation's grants would target disadvantaged youth growing up in challenged neighborhoods. This was something that had not been targeted regularly before.

Two years later, the Winged O Foundation ran its first fundraising golf tournament. Funds from the tournament and other Winged O fundraising efforts were allocated to athletic programs for disadvantaged youth. I was chairman of the golf committee for the first several years. The first year of the tournament netted over $100k for the programs the foundation supported. Every year of the tournament after that was equally successful. Early on, Earl Woods and his aspiring pro golfer son, Tiger, attended the Winged O Tournament as my guests.

The Foundation has funded capital projects such as the refurbishing of the Ernest Ingold swimming pool in the

Haight Ashbury district of San Francisco, the resurfacing of the tennis courts at Golden Gate Park, and the creation and/or refurbishing of school playgrounds throughout the Bay Area. Also, the foundation funds sports programs, such as after-school basketball leagues in Oakland and Alameda County, a girls soccer team in San Mateo County, the First Tee Program for junior golfers, San Francisco Little League, and the Junior Giants. The foundation also funds the purchase of needed sports equipment such as uniforms, bats, balls, nets, and scoreboards to communities that are in need.

Each year, I leveraged my nationwide network of contacts to get friends from all over the country to sign up and play in the tournament – which helped the tournament sell out, year after year. Because so many African Americans showed up to play, it quietly became referred to as the "Car Wash" by a handful of other club members. I actually thought the car wash reference was hilarious and had privately joked with a couple of my closest friends about adding some chamois cloth drying towels to our tournament gift bag, but I was just joking, of course.

Today, the foundation's grants continue to help young athletes learn very important lifelong lessons. We believe it is through competition on the athletic field, on the golf courses, on the tennis courts, in the pool, on the track, on the squash, handball and racquetball courts, on the gymnasium floor, and in other athletic venues that kids first learn about commitment, sportsmanship, fair play, teamwork, leadership, and trust. The Olympic Club Foundation has provided millions of dollars for athletic programs for disadvantaged Bay Area youth.

Through my work and leadership with the foundation, I was able to get one of my baseball heroes, Baseball Hall of Famer and San Francisco Giants great, Willie Mays, to support the foundation. He came to play at our annual golf tournament and became a donor. That was amazing, but the most fascinating thing is that he became a good friend. I actually helped him become a member of the Olympic Club based on my recommendation. Can you imagine? I helped Willie Mays, the "Say Hey Kid", maybe the greatest all-around baseball player ever, when he applied for membership to the club. That's not all. The club was high class, no doubt about that, but there were two locker room areas. One was the general area, and then there was a special room that was available to the board of directors and longtime club members. When Mays joined, he was given a locker in the usual locker room for newcomers, despite his celebrity status. How could that be possible? It was like giving a birdcage to an eagle.

I quickly brought it to the attention of my fellow board of directors. They agreed that no celebrity of his status should be assigned to the general locker room, and they promised to get him in the upscale room as soon as possible. I decided to let him share my locker until the change was finalized. For several months, the name on my locker read, "Roy Clay/Willie Mays". We became good friends, and sometimes we would just sit there, laughing and talking about everything until our faces hurt. He told me about his secret on how to hit a curveball once, but he made me swear not to tell anyone, and I never did. I even learned that we were very similar in how we were raised, with very little, except values, work ethic, and the will to be the best. If someone had told me that this was going to happen earlier in my life, I would have questioned their sanity. However, it happened at the Olympic Club, and it wasn't a dream, just another unbelievable moment in my life. Things were not always perfect for me, especially considering some of the difficulties dealing with racism, and the toughest of all, seeing my wife battle cancer. Still, there were always times throughout my life when I felt like the luckiest man in the world.

Over the years, the club became a great place for me to bond with two of my sons, Rodney and Chris since both enjoyed playing golf. I was so proud of how they fit in with the guys, and they were not bad on the golf course, either. They were also thrilled to know Willie Mays and enjoyed chatting with him. I was a proud dad when they got together with me to play and socialize in the clubhouse at least a few times a month. When we were on the golf course together, I always joked around with them saying, "These folks couldn't keep me from joining the club and playing golf on this course, but I always remembered not to dig around alone over in the bushes for my ball too long." After a while in the rough, it was just another lost ball. I think I was buying more golf balls than any member that played that course. My sons and I tried to make light of things like that, but the truth is that we did have to be more observant of things like that because of our race, and based on their past experiences, my sons were very aware of it. Unfortunately, it was always a reality for black men when visiting white spaces.

I must emphasize, again, that I joined the Olympic Club, not as a protest, but simply because I wanted to play regularly on the best golf course available. I remained an active member for nearly two decades before I could no longer play golf, well, due to my age. While there were a few detractors in the club, I had many friends there, guys who would do anything for me, and I was always treated well by every single staff member - from bartenders to the head golf pro. "When you walk with someone, something unspoken happens." Those are the words of Sidney Poitier when reflecting on his many experiences as the only black person on a movie set, or at a meeting. That quote reminds me of when I was the only person of color moving around in the clubhouse or walking the fairways of the golf course. In most cases, we learned to match each other's pace and respect each other's individuality, more from just observing than from words being spoken. In most cases, that helped us become better people. After all these years, I am overwhelmed with pride when I speak of my membership in the Olympic Club, especially being the first African American to do so. I was also honored to be a member of the board of directors when we opened the club to women members in 1990. I smiled last year when it was announced that the Olympic Club would host the 2033 Ryder Cup.

In front of the Lake Course 18th green and clubhouse of the Olympic Club

Chapter Ten

LOSING VIRGINIA

It was the 1990s, George H.W. Bush was our president, and America had fought another war, yet again. The Persian Gulf War didn't last long, though. It began in August 1990, after Iraq's invasion of Kuwait, in a bid to gain more control over the lucrative oil supply in the Middle East. The U.S. and the United Nations demanded that Iraq, led by Saddam Hussein, withdraw troops, but Hussein refused. Sounds familiar right, except the United States and a coalition of 34 countries began a bombing campaign against key Iraqi locations, followed by a ground force attack called Operation Desert Storm. In the end, Hussein signed a cease-fire agreement and released Kuwait in February of 1992. It was a victory for us, but we lost well over 4,000 soldiers during that war, and more than 31,000 were injured. You could not help but feel sorrow for the fellow Americans and their families who were among the casualties of war. Fortunately for me, none of those persons lost were my family members, but there were those in our community who had lost loved ones.

Coincidentally, this was a time when Virginia and I were giving a lot of thought to our own mortality again, so when we saw an abundant loss of life during that war it definitely hit home with us, and also gave us more appreciation for life itself.

Also, my close associate and good friend, Tom Perkins, was an early investor and incubator of one of the world's leading cancer drug development companies, Genentech. Tom promised that he could make any of those new and experimental products available to Virginia with a mere phone call. We would have access to cutting-edge treatments, but after giving it some thought, Virginia and I both opted not to go that route. However, we did have the privilege of meeting some of the world's top cancer researchers through our connection with Genentech. Tom's altruism, combined with our long friendship with the experts at the Palo Alto Medical Foundation, a leading institute in cancer research where, again, I had proudly served as a board member, enabled us to receive all the advice possible about making Virginia more comfortable. That was just as important to us.

I was starting to sit back and reflect on the experiences of my life more often now, almost every day it seemed. I suspect the rigors of staying competitive in Silicon Valley and caring for my ailing wife had taken a toll on me. Maybe it was just a matter of age catching up with me. After all, by this time, I had taken more than sixty trips around the sun, and I had a few more gray hairs to show for it. My experiences and

accomplishments were more than I could have imagined as a kid growing up back in Kinloch. However, great things always seemed to happen for me, and there was no stopping me once I got started with something. Caring for my spouse, whose very life was depending on me, was a daunting and strenuous task, but nothing had ever been more gratifying for me than comforting my loving wife and helping her feel just a little better on those not-so-good days. If the situation was reversed, I know she would have done much more for me. Thankfully, the caregiver counseling and advice I received prepared me for the emotionally difficult times I was experiencing.

After a long day of meetings, mentoring, and planning, I would often sit at my desk at the ROD-L office, lean back, and take a deep breath. In those fleeting moments of relaxation, I reflected on all the gratifying success that had come my way. Yes, I had big dreams, but I never imagined becoming a leader, in the eyes of so many whose careers I was responsible for getting started. I didn't like being called "the godfather" initially, but as I rocked back in that black leather chair, I felt the realization of how much I had impacted the lives of dozens of young men and women. Then I felt deserving of the title, "Godfather of Silicon Valley," as I was affectionately called. I also thought about the leadership I was currently providing to the Olympic Club Foundation and my vision for organizing more to help those who were underserved. I remembered, "To whom much is given, much is expected" and that is what kept me from becoming complacent, as there was always more to get done. It was a good life, but it did come without some extremely difficult times, like dealing with the lifelong challenge of overcoming discrimination and helping my wife and best friend through her battle with cancer.

We already knew that Virginia's prognosis was terminal, but in November of 1993, we were called to her doctor's office for a sit-down meeting for an update on her status. Upon arriving, I sat close to Virginia on a beautifully upholstered printed couch. I held her hand and remarked at how immaculate and colorful the waiting area was that day. She grinned, agreeing with me, and responded, "This place always has that bright and clean feeling of home." All the while, I'm sure she realized that my intention was to relax her and myself on this otherwise sun-filled California day. The mood changed quickly, however, as we could tell from the look in the doctor's eyes that the news was not going to be good. The doctor looked at us, and with his voice trembling, informed us that Virginia only had a few months to live. I couldn't breathe after hearing those words. I was as close to being in a state of shock as I ever thought possible. I wanted to comfort her, but the words were not there. That moment did not seem real at the time, but I still remember it vividly, as if it was yesterday. I wanted to be strong for Virginia, but I felt helpless. I tried to hold back the tears, and then she held me tightly and said, "Don't worry. Our love is here to stay." She was referring to our favorite song. I agreed, and we squeezed each other for minutes. After controlling our tears, we thought about how we would tell our sons. It took a while to sink in, but after a couple of days, she and I both finally came to grips with her fate, and we had a talk with our sons. When they were told that no further treatment would cure their mom or keep her alive, they were saddened and disheartened. We were not really a group hug type of family, but we held each other this time, and there were more tears. We all decided that Virginia and I would telephone other family members to inform them. We also devised a plan to be with her at all times, and at least one of us would always be at her bedside, keeping her company.

Virginia was already ordering 'Meals on Wheels' for us most days so that we did not have to worry about having nutritious food in the house. It was amazing to watch her carefully make those orders with our health and our favorite dishes in mind. It was just her way, like when she was a teenager taking care of her siblings while her mother was working two jobs. No matter what, we ensured she was never alone, which seemed to keep her interested and wanting to stay with us as long as it was humanly possible. It was either the boys or me, and sometimes her sister would drive down the coast and stay with her for a weekend. This was our way of making sure she was never alone, despite our busy schedules. It was also a way for each of us to get a deeper understanding of what she was going through and give her some personalized attention in our own respective ways.

It was no coincidence that we were able to do this because we had our own business. That goes back to the decisions I made in the past when I turned down higher-paying positions that were offered to me so that I could run my own business. Spending time with my family was more important to me than anything, and I did not want someone telling me that work should come before caring for my wife. There were many managers who did not see the value of their employees' family lives, so I always said to my sons, "There is nothing worse than working for a damn fool!"

Some days Virginia was in good spirits, and others, she was not, as one would expect. One Saturday, after I returned home from playing a round of golf at the club, Virginia greeted me, then looked me square in the eyes and asked if I would find a minister that she could talk to. That surprised me, but without hesitation, I replied with a "yes," although I did not know how I would deliver on her request at the time. After all, I had not attended a regular church service for more than 50 years, so knowing Virginia, she probably thought that it was time for me to get in touch with my spirituality as well. As usual, she appeared confident I would make her request a reality.

Later that week, a young black man requested to meet with me in my ROD-L office in Menlo Park. He had heard about my successful business career, and it was his desire that I voluntarily provide some occasional career guidance to Black students at Stanford University. I replied, yes, without hesitation, not knowing yet, that he was a minister. I knew that Virginia would be pleased with me giving that kind of assistance because my life had been devoted to giving advice and assistance to young people of color since 1965.

When we met at the office to discuss his idea in person, I noticed that he wore a clergy collar. He introduced himself as Reverend Floyd Thompkins, Assistant to the Chaplain of the Stanford University Church. It was nothing short of a miracle. I paused briefly, wondering, *How could this be true?* Within a few minutes, we discussed the details of my participation in his program. I then mentioned my family to him and took a moment to describe my wife's medical situation to him. He appeared sincerely concerned and asked if there was some way that he could help me. I told him that she had recently requested to speak to a minister. He told me he would be glad to talk with Virginia anytime we needed him. So, the miracle of Reverend Thompkins had begun as he visited our home and talked weekly with Virginia.

Virginia was becoming more confined to our bedroom, and television was a way for her to stay connected with what was happening in the world and be entertained simultaneously. Soon she became fascinated with the events surrounding the OJ Simpson trial that had captivated the nation. She watched it daily with whoever was sitting with her. You would have thought she was the judge herself. She was not alone, though, as millions of others were emotionally drawn to the case by the initial drama of that long memorable day in June of 1994 when the world paused just a little. My brother, Charles, said that even his friends at the assembly lines stopped making cars in Detroit for a few minutes to catch a glimpse of the spectacle. That is when the here-to-fore beloved Simpson, who went from football stardom to actor and broadcaster, became the object of that infamous low-speed pursuit in his friend, Al Cowling's Ford Bronco after Simpson did not turn himself in when he was charged with the murders of his ex-wife Nicole Brown Simpson and her friend Ron Goldman.

I was at the Olympic Club when Simpson was being chased by the police that day. Everyone at the club, staff and members, stopped what they were doing to witness the breathtaking action that was on display, in living color, you could say, on national television. My memory is not so good now, but I think we were seeing right before our eyes something that had never been witnessed live by millions of viewers and onlookers. It was something to see a celebrity like Simpson, in the back of that SUV, with a gun to his head, being pursued by siren-flashing police cruisers, and being cheered on by fans who were gathering at every corner, it seemed, some yelling, "Go OJ, go." We realized almost immediately that this time he was not acting in a movie scene, or one of those popular television commercials running through airports. I noticed that the club members around me were chanting, "Just shoot him." All of them were white. I was the only one who seemed to have empathy for OJ that day. Not that I was in any way sure of his innocence, it was just a matter of compassion for another human being and hoping he would live through this ordeal with an opportunity to fairly defend the charges against him. That is all a man can ask, and that is the only way we would know the truth.

The actions of my friends at the clubhouse show how white and black folks differed in opinion regarding whether OJ, a black man, was innocent or not of killing two white victims. People say the country is split now, but I contend that this was an example of how we have always viewed issues like this differently, especially how we see things along racial or color lines. After seeing so many blacks die at the hands of police in my life, I was hoping for a better outcome this time. I felt a little lonely among my fellow club members that afternoon, so I headed home, despite wanting to hang on to every minute of that compelling television coverage. I resumed watching the coverage with Virginia after arriving home safely and making sure she was comfortable. We discussed the events until late that night and almost every day afterward.

Throughout the lengthy trial, we were interested in this case just like everyone else, but Virginia said her interest went deeper. We were on both sides of how we hoped to see things handled, especially when considering a prior situation with our son Rodney. When Rodney was younger, he got himself into some trouble, but fortunately, he got off with a slap on the wrist because I could afford a top-level attorney. That was not normally available to many people of color, and it still isn't. There were several questions that are still asked about the events surrounding this memorable case. First, was OJ framed because he was black? Secondly, did he get off as innocent because he could afford top-level legal representation? And lastly, why was he not shot on the freeway during the chase like what has become all too familiar for the average black person?

Simpson was represented by the high-profile defense team referred to as the "Dream Team," which was initially led by Robert Shapiro, and subsequently directed by Johnnie Cochran. The latter may have been the best black defense attorney of his time. The team also included F. Lee Bailey, Alan Dershowitz, Robert Kardashian, Shawn Holley, Carl E. Douglas, and Gerald Helmen. Barry Scheck and Peter Neufeld were two additional attorneys who specialized in DNA evidence. That was some team, and Simpson had the bank account to afford it.

The trial went on for months, with many jaw-dropping moments, but none that will stick out as much as Johnnie Cochran's initial statement, "If the glove don't fit, you must acquit," after Simpson demonstrated in court that his hand was too large to fit the blood-stained glove found on his property by police officers. That statement was so impactful as it appeared that Cochran was speaking as a *voice straight from the hood* in that first statement, but he later changed the statement to, "If it doesn't fit, you must acquit," in his closing argument. Cochran was also able to convince the jury that there was reasonable doubt concerning the DNA evidence in this case, which was a relatively new form of evidence in trials at that time. There were mixed emotions across the country as many who followed the case did not agree with the verdict.

Virginia never stated whether or not she thought Simpson was guilty or innocent, but I have a feeling she knew after watching so many hours of testimony and arguments during her last year with us. It was her own big soap opera, or better yet, it was reality television in the making. Sometimes I think that trial was the entertainment that was keeping her alive longer than the doctor had predicted. Reverend Thompkins's weekly chats and our tender loving care didn't hurt either. She was enjoying and appreciating every bit of life that she had left.

Just before the verdict was given, Virginia's health took another downward turn. She had lost a lot of weight fast, and her appearance was frail now. She had not been able to eat and all she could consume was Ensure, the nutritional drink, which, over time, just wasn't enough. She was admitted back into the hospital, and this time she was assigned to hospice with no hope of surviving more than a month. She asked if it would be more convenient for me if she spent her last days in the hospital. I emphatically responded, "No, we want you with us at home." The boys echoed my response, as we wanted her last thoughts to be that she came first to us.

On one occasion, while Virginia was still in her hospital room, before finishing the hospice period at home, she expressed that she was not feeling good about herself as a woman, which is not unusual for breast cancer patients. I leaned over and gently kissed and embraced her as intimately as was possible in that setting. I wanted her to know how appealing she was to me. I said, "You're still beautiful in my eyes, Virginia". She smacked me on my hand and said, "Roy, how can I be beautiful? Look at my hair and this hospital gown; I haven't worn makeup in days, and I'm so skinny." I squeezed her hand, looked into her eyes, and whispered, "That's not what beauty is. Beauty is your genuine loving heart and your beautiful soul. The look in your eyes when you greet me each day. It's the way you affectionately lay your head on my shoulder, and it will always be the way you make me feel just watching you walk into a room, just like the first time I saw you." She gave me that familiar look, and I looked back. She smiled, laid her head on my shoulder and slowly drifted off to sleep. "And suddenly all your troubles melt away, all your worries are gone, and it is for no reason other than the look in your partner's eyes. Yes, sometimes life and love really is that simple." Those words from William Wordsworth say it all, and I was thinking, *Virginia was alright now.*

It was great getting her home again those last few weeks. My staff at ROD-L stepped up to the plate and were so kind and loyal to me at a time when I needed them the most. We even got a few visits from them as well. I think they knew that I would not do any less for them if they needed me, based on my family-first management style. Towards the end, there was a steady procession of friends and family that came to visit, which helped me and my sons a lot.

One of the keys to keeping the family level-headed and comfortable during Virginia's last year was the involvement of Reverend Thompkins. Let me begin by saying God sent Reverend Thompkins to me at the right time. While growing up in Kinloch, I was the son of a part-time Baptist minister. My eight siblings were baptized as Christians in the church, but I was the child who refused to become a Christian. I had a good reason not to, in my mind. All nine of my daddy's children walked about a mile each Sunday morning to arrive for a 9:30 am Sunday School service. However, located about half that distance in the opposite direction, there was a "Whites only" Baptist church.

One Sunday, I felt it was time to introduce myself to those people. It looked like a nice place from the outside, but I had no idea what was inside that place that was twice the size of our church. Somehow, I had the curiosity and the courage to walk across the street we were not supposed to cross. Once I was on the other side, there was no stopping my little self. I was all of about 95 pounds, and a good gust of wind would have blown me over back in those days. I just had to see inside that church. It must be made of gold or something since they only allowed white folks inside. I took a deep breath and hurried up the steps behind some white folks and their children as I attempted to attend their church service. Maybe they would let me in because I did not look threatening. I thought someone would have to feel sorry for me, right? After all, they were Christians.

I looked up at that tall, shiny steeple, hoping for a blessing that morning, and stepped boldly inside the open church door. The male usher was conversing with an older woman and didn't notice me at first. I vividly remember the stares and whispers coming from a few bystanders as I stood just behind the back row of the church pews. Then there was a feeling, like when a thick cloud covers the sun, that had come over me, and it certainly did not feel like God was anywhere around. That was when the crew cut burly usher tapped me on the shoulder. The next thing I knew is that I was refused attendance and escorted out like something less than a human. "Go on boy. Didn't your parents tell you that coloreds aren't allowed in a white church?" I wanted to respond with something like, "But it's not a white church. It's God's church." However, since I didn't seem to be getting any backup from God, I held my breath and left the premises. I was hurt and humiliated and felt like I was crying on the inside as much as the tears that were rolling down my face while making my way home. That incident made me feel so bad that I did not eat supper that afternoon.

After that rejection, I told my father that I refused to serve the same being as the members of that "Whites only" church. Therefore, I no longer wished to go to church. I told him I would rather play baseball on Sundays. He accepted my decision. My mother, also a devout Christian, did not agree with my thinking. Still, she supported me, and even washed and folded my baseball uniform for each Sunday. I have had many successful instances of being the *first black,* but it didn't happen at that (Whites Only) church that Sunday, and it obviously left a bad taste in my mouth that night and deep into my adulthood.

I thought I would never get over the traumatic rejection at that Ferguson church, but Reverend Thompkins's presence later in my life made me a believer again. I was not only just hopeful, but he showed me how to have faith as well. My faith that I could handle whatever happened next was tested when Virginia's battle with cancer was coming closer to the end. I remember when they induced her into a coma after being at home under hospice care for almost two weeks. At this point, we mostly just sat and watched her breathe for the last week or so. Here was the woman I shared so much of my life with, who inspired me, loved me, and shared so many of life's moments with me. It was hard to see her lying there motionless, with no way of responding to us, but still alive. The doctor assured us that she was comfortable, but that didn't make it any easier to see her in that unrecoverable state of mind and body.

Chris was at her bedside the moment that she stopped breathing. He said he saw her chest rise and fall one last time, and then he called out to me after she breathed her last breath at 9:30 pm on February 16, 1995. I raced in from another room and checked her pulse, and said to Chris, "She's gone." I kissed her and cried quietly, pulled the sheet over her, and called the coroner. Chris called Rodney and

Roy, who were not far away, and they came back to the house immediately. Although her passing was expected, we were all extremely devastated. No amount of preparation could have fully prepared us for this, as we would never see her warm smile or hear her calming voice again. All we had now were memories.

We all took turns calling family, our closest friends, and notifying Reverend Thompkins. In parallel with the time Reverend Thompkins was counseling Virginia in those last days of hospice, I had been consulting with the local mortician, Charles Jones, to prepare for her death. I called him that night, as well. The next day, a photographer friend just happened to come to my house with a special photograph of Virginia and me. It is a picture that I still cherish, the last that we took together. I connected Reverend Thompkins with Charles Jones, the mortician, and began to plan her memorial with the help of our closest friends that next day. The next few days were exhausting, days I will always remember. I slept for no more than 10 hours the entire week.

My mind was still somewhat dazed when Reverend Thompkins called to inform me that he would conduct her memorial service at none other than the Stanford Memorial Church, located on the university's campus. It was truly an honor, and I hope he realized my gratitude for going out of his way to do that for us. After all, this was the first time a ceremony of this kind had been held there for a black woman. The day of her service was as big as we had ever seen in our city. There was not an empty parking space within a half-mile. The Palo Alto City Council adjourned its meeting in her honor that day. The Palo Alto Police Chief, Jim Zurcher, closed the main highway, University Avenue, leading to Stanford, in order to relieve the anticipated traffic congestion. In an unbelievable display of honor and respect, the Police Chief was in his formal dress uniform. He directed traffic himself that seasonably cool, but uncharacteristically bright February day, and personally drove anyone of our family who wished assistance, to the chapel, in his vehicle.

The chapel was filled to capacity with people from all occupations and social classes, including the Palo Alto Mayor, City staff and Councilmembers, the president, and members of the Board of The Olympic Club of San Francisco; all of whom witnessed the most beautiful ceremony I could have ever conceived. Reverend Thompkins conducted the memorial service with heartfelt dignity. He had become our brother during Virginia's battle. This wonderful celebration of life concluded with a repast at the prestigious Stanford Faculty Club that was made possible by a friend. The ceremony ended with our song, "Our Love Is Here to Stay." February 23, 1995, ended the longest yet most beautiful day of my life. It was all made possible thanks to the good Reverend Floyd Thompkins, who miraculously came into our lives right when we needed him. Virginia would have been pleased.

The mortician cremated Virginia's body, and her ashes were strewn over the same Pacific Ocean that she marveled at when we first arrived in California. The special place she loved to visit. Furthermore, our sons were so distraught that I did not want them, nor me, to view her ravaged body at a funeral. I also felt that Virginia's ashes vanishing into the wind and suspended eternally in the air, made it feel like she would be with me wherever I went.

It saddened me to see Virginia suffer so much that last year. I doubt that I could have been enough for her during that struggle had it not been for my amazing sons, who were always there, physically and emotionally, when I could not be. She was a steadfast family-first person, as shown by her encouraging me to pursue my dream as an entrepreneur, which also allowed me the flexibility to spend more time with family. A second mom to almost all of our son's friends, she welcomed them to our home and often cooked lunch or dinner for them.

Together, she and I instilled the value of education in our sons. She was also committed to giving back to the underserved in the community as well. As a founder of The Boys and Girls Club of the Mid-Peninsula in East Palo Alto, she asked me to continue serving as president of The Girls Club of the Mid-Peninsula and bringing a little sunshine into the lives of others who were not as well off as we were. That was vintage Virginia, always putting others first.

A clear example of her devotion to the family is her request that my sons and I stay close to each other. She felt that we were never as strong as when we were together. In our last conversations, there was a lot of reflection and even laughter about our early years as a couple and about our children's childhood experiences. Our sons and I also thanked her back for her love and devotion, and for always being such a strong advocate and supporter of us all. It simply would not have been a household without Virginia as a wife, mother, and matriarch.

One humorous note is that Rodney was always late to everything. He was late to family dinners, outings, and parties. Whatever it was, he was late. So, in the midst of the most difficult time of Virginia's final days managing our household, her funniest request to all of us was, "Make sure Rodney isn't late to my memorial service!" This is an example of how she kept our family together. At that point in her life, it was sort of like, *the bottom of the ninth with two outs and nobody on base*," and she still had a sense of humor during her last days. She knew she would get some smiles and laughter out of us, and she did. We teased Rodney the next day, and we laughed again. That's just another small example of the joy Virginia brought into our lives.

Virginia Clay, July 1929 – February 1995

Chapter Eleven

THIS LIFE GOES ON

It goes without saying that the first few years of life after Virginia were as difficult as any time I can remember. It seemed like a part of me had gone with her. We had become like one person, more than I had ever realized, and that other half of me was no longer there. Waking up to those typical cool, foggy Bay Area mornings with her beside me began to feel like so long ago. She was my morning cup of coffee with a hint of cream and brown sugar, and the bright ray of sunshine gently opening up my rested eyes. She was also the sound of the soft night rain that calmed, rejuvenated, and prepared me for the next challenging day. For nearly four decades, she had my back in a very unforgiving, competitive, and often unfair world, supporting my every dream, vision, and aspiration. Simply put, she was everything to me.

As time went on, I slowly began to develop skills that involved managing the household, with Roy, Jr and Rodney assisting me since they were living at the house at that time. It was not easy to handle the household chores and manage my company simultaneously. Planning meals and keeping my clothes clean are two examples, but her calm demeanor, confidence, tenacity, and pep talks when I needed them were also missed. All this while grieving the loss of this woman, the love of my life.

That day in 1995, when I lost Virginia, was the longest day of the longest week of my life. More than a year later, as I was looking through a family photo album, I remember thinking of a promise that I had made to her that was still just as meaningful to me as it was the day I softly whispered it in her ear. I told her that our love would stay in my heart as long as I could breathe, and that promise still resonates with me today. While thumbing through those dozens of photographs in that album, I noticed the smiles we had on our faces in most of the images. They were warm, happy smiles that reflected our love. Back then, the question in my mind was, *why was our love so special?*

I was asked that question by friends who wanted to know our secret so they could strengthen their relationships back in the day. I did not have the answer then, but I have since described love as being synonymous with respect. When there is love, respect must follow somewhere close behind it if love is to thrive and last forever. While love is an affection felt towards a person, respect is an admiration that bonds the relationship. Love can fade away at times, but as long as respect is given and received by both persons, that love will likely succeed. That was certainly true for us. She would say, "Let me see your sample ballot to make sure I am voting the same." We would discuss differences, which were rare, and resolve those differences.

There was one statement by her that I will always remember. I still think of it now. When she was a young woman, she said to me, "I like being with you more than any person I have ever known because you are bright, you have earned respect from so many people, and you are so much fun to be with. This confirms the intuition that led me to want to know you when I first heard about you." Those are the words of a woman who knew what she wanted in a life partner. It was fascinating that she had so much respect and admiration for me.

I was fortunate to have a wife who believed in me until the end. She always kept my level of tenacity at a high level, which kept me motivated and confident that I could achieve anything. That meant so much to me. Her admiration for me is why she thought I should tell the story of my life. She probably realized that I would not have done it unless she helped to get me started, and she put her heart into doing just that. There were many newspaper articles and pictures that she had saved and organized in chronological order. There were articles from my election to the Palo Alto City Council, and stories and features about me becoming the first black Vice Mayor in Palo Alto. She also had newspaper clippings from my groundbreaking admittance to the Olympic Club, and there were numerous notes I had written regarding my leadership in the development of the computer division at HP, and journals that I wrote after I became an entrepreneur. She also compiled a comprehensive list of telephone numbers and addresses of important business associates and acquaintances.

I tried to work on more anecdotes for the book whenever I had free time or wasn't playing golf. I was actually enjoying it too. Virginia had given me that good head start on the project, so I was committed to following through.

In the early 90s, a lifelong friend of Chris and Rodney, Andre Chapman, started a youth development organization called The Unity Care Group. The organization has been a great resource and service to thousands of disadvantaged youths in the Bay Area over the years. Chris and I are both proud to have served on Unity Care's board of directors for many years. In the late 90s, I partnered with the Unity Care Group to start the Virginia Clay / Unity Care Group Golf Classic, a golf tournament to raise money for Unity Care's youth science and engineering program. The tournament ran for several years and was a great success in raising money for the program. I was so proud of how my sons and I worked together, along with the other tournament committee members, to make this event successful each year, and I was sure that Virginia was watching over us and pleased as well.

Sometimes I feel like just sitting in my favorite chair and taking a nap, then there are other times I sit there and think about my life. I think mostly about the things I've seen, the things I have accomplished, and the relationships I have made over the years. I think about my mother and my dear

Virginia and all that they have meant to me. Everything I became was because of them. When I look up to the stars, as the still of the night finally reaches the West Coast, I close my eyes and think of them. Then I feel them smiling down and driving me to continue, as long as I can, to help make this world better.

I hope they are happy with the way the boys and I have stayed together as a family. I also hope they approve of the life I have lived despite missing their help and encouragement these last decades as we are now halfway through the year 2022, some twenty-seven years removed from Virginia's passing as I complete this chapter. It's a tough thing when you lose the people who helped push you and mold you. Those are the people who help you get right when you get off track and who keep you on the right path, sometimes without even speaking a word. I wish my fortunes of having a good mother and supportive spouse to everyone who has big dreams and ambitious goals they are passionate about. I must say that the old *thinking chair* sure does get a lot more use now than it did in my more youthful days.

I still recall how decades before Steve Jobs and Bill Gates started the personal computer revolution, I began working at the Livermore National Laboratory. I was responsible for developing a computing platform the size of 100 refrigerators that tracked radiation diffusion in the event of an atom bomb exploding in the Bay Area. As mentioned earlier, that was the beginning of this life in business and technology that has defined me after moving to a part of the country that would later be considered the center of the western world. I had no idea it would one day be called Silicon Valley, the home of huge companies like Apple, Facebook, and Google, whose headquarters are here. This was also where it all began for Hewlett-Packard (HP). Who would have known that the Cupertino plot of land I helped identify and secure for Hewlett Packard would eventually become Apple Computer's famous "Spaceship" Apple Park headquarters? I am so grateful when I think back to those days.

Over the years, I have received many honors from the likes of the United Negro College Fund (UNCF) for giving opportunities and mentoring to graduates of HBCUs, and honors from other charitable and community-based organizations. One of the recognitions that I am most proud of is being inducted into the Silicon Valley Engineering Council's Hall of Fame in 2003. It was my Mount Rushmore event. I was honored, not for being the first black, but purely for my excellent pioneering professional accomplishments. I had become a Hall of Famer and had joined the man who I credit with my start in the tech industry, David Packard, as well as Bill Hewlett and other hi-tech luminaries. I was always very proud of my work, and now it was very satisfying to know that others in the industry had also recognized my contributions.

In the early 2000s, I and a group of Silicon Valley-based black businessmen, who were friends and colleagues, formed a group. We were all, well, "seasoned", so we fittingly called our group the Old Black Guys (OBGs). Meetings were held monthly and still are. It was always clearly stated that we would meet with no plan or hidden agendas. Our purpose was to meet only to catch up with what was current in the Bay Area and share the stories of our struggles, challenges, and successes. Of course, there would often be a member who would recommend a new remedy for joint or back pain, and that always seemed to be of interest to the group members. Over the years, members have included many longtime family friends, golfing buddies, and business associates, with a broad range of professional backgrounds from technology executives to attorneys, to executives in large nonprofits.

Some of the group members include Ken Coleman, John Thompson, Bill Green, Carl Banks, John Templeton, Harold Boyd, Hugh Burroughs, Jim Knight, Harry Bremond, and several others that I had bonded with over the years. Just to mention a couple of them, John Thompson, considered one of the most brilliant executives in Silicon Valley, is currently the chair of Illumina, past chair of Microsoft, and before that he had been a vice president at IBM. It's also important to note that he is an HBCU graduate, with an undergraduate degree from Florida A&M University. Ken Coleman was a founder, chairman and CEO of ITM Software, a Silicon Valley software company. He first landed in the valley in 1972 after a stint as an Air Force officer. Someone recommended him to me, and I introduced him to HP where he held several management positions; as he says, "The rest is history." He considers me a mentor who inspired him because there were few black executives in the valley when he arrived. He became known for his excellent recruiting skills and is still an expert in diversity and inclusion. He sits on the boards of many companies in an advisory role today and has received many honors, including induction into the Global Silicon Valley Hall of Fame.

These were all strong, brilliant, very accomplished men in their own right. The common denominator was that we were black and had succeeded against the odds. You can imagine some of the stories that were told and discussions that were raised on those Thursday afternoons. So much wisdom was shared, and it was always a time to release some similar frustrations, no matter what our fields of endeavor might have been. It was our way to take a deep breath and lift each other up as men. Great ideas came about as a result of those meetings as well, especially those relating to giving back to those who were from our marginalized and underserved communities. OBG members didn't have to join our group at this stage of their lives, but they did, and for that and all they accomplished in life, they are all true godfathers in my book.

I contributed to one particularly funny moment at one of the OBG gatherings. It was a breezy, Thursday afternoon, and when it was my turn to speak, I realized that I didn't have anything current to talk about, so I reached back and told a story about how my son was racially profiled while trying to purchase donuts for a meeting that I had at my office with Reverend Jesse Jackson in the late 1990s.

Jesse had stopped by my Rod-L Electronics offices in Menlo Park to meet with me. It was still mid-morning, so I sent my son Rodney out to buy donuts for Jesse and his staff to go along with the premium coffee we brewed ourselves at the office. I gave Rodney a $100 bill to purchase them at the nationally known grocery chain located close by. When he tried to pay them with the $100 bill, the cashier called the manager over, and they detained Rodney, locking the store doors so he couldn't run away. So essentially, Rodney was racially profiled while trying to run an errand for me to provide for Jesse Jackson and his team of staffers. When Rodney was finally released, he returned to the office and told us what had happened. I was furious and so was Jesse. Some of his staff thought it was quite ironic that Jesse was there to witness it. We all thought it was hilarious and a bit unlucky for the store manager to racially profile a young man running an errand for Jesse Jackson. We laughed a bit, and one of the staffers said to Jackson, "This is another good opportunity for you to show America how we are still treated unfairly, sir."

I called the store manager and asked him to return my $100 bill and told him that we did not wish to purchase the donuts after the racial profiling had occurred. The manager drove over and returned my money, but who did he see sitting there in my office but Jesse Jackson and his team. The look on his face was priceless. He apologized to us in about as many ways as there were donuts in that box that he now insisted were compliments of the grocery chain. It was incredibly bad luck for that grocery chain, as the incident made its way into a wide-spread media campaign. I even received a call from the grocery chain's CEO one evening apologizing for the incident. Later, that CEO made a public apology for his employee's mistake. Unfortunately, this is another example of what we have to cope with as Black Americans every day - no matter who or where we are.

Although it had been reported by the news media some years before, my friends never let me live my version of the story down after I told it. My guess is that they are probably still laughing about the way I described the look on that grocery store manager's face when he showed up at my office and there was none other than civil rights icon, Reverend Jesse Jackson.

Recently, I thought about the challenges of being a black man in America. I reflected on how James Baldwin described it as "affecting a man's sanity" when I was being interviewed on camera not too long ago. It was just the interviewer and me sitting on stools across from each other in an otherwise empty room. Kathy Cotton was the interviewer, and not only did I know her, but she is well known in the Bay Area. At the end of the segment, I was asked, "What was the greatest challenge in your life, Mr. Clay?" I didn't quite hear the question, initially, and asked Kathy to repeat the question. She repeated, "What was the greatest challenge in your life?" I understood her very well this time. I paused for a second, looked her directly in the eye, and responded, "racism" then after pausing for a couple of seconds, I repeated my answer even more emphatically, "Yes, dealing with racism for sure." Kathy is a mature, experienced black woman who knew exactly what I meant by that answer. She seemed to hold back some emotions, and it is evident that between the two of us, we had dealt with more discrimination and unfair treatment than we cared to discuss at that moment, but we knew it had to be said. Then she said, "I can imagine what you have faced after being born a black child in a segregated society, but that is why your story needs to be told so all Americans will know the truths that must not be repeated." I thought about what my family and I had endured during my lifetime. I said, "Racism is the worst thing in the world...we are quick to say that we are a nation that stands for freedom, but I'm talking about a group of people who have been deprived of equality, and that is what I have experienced in my lifetime." She nodded, as if agreeing, and then wrapped up the interview.

If the segment went further, and had she asked what could be done about racism, I probably would have said, "We cannot change it unless we face the fact that it is a problem," which is also taken from something James Baldwin wrote. Race relations are a lot better now than they were decades ago, but we still have a long way to go. I am looking forward to the day that all Americans look in the mirror, face this societal ill, and make the changes that will make us truly indivisible, where the only thing that matters is love for each other. I want to know what that looks like, sounds like, and feels like. I would have told her that, although I am old now,

I still have dreams and hopes for a better future. That being said, my kids and grandkids have the same mentality that I did back in the 50s and 60s – nothing is going to stop them from achieving their goals.

I have participated in several interviews like that in the last 15 years, and I have enjoyed them all. Speaking to groups of students and sometimes to young aspiring professionals in the technology field has always been a part of me, and I still have a thirst for it.

Several years ago, my body could no longer swing a golf club, so I had to stop playing. That was hard to do. The game of golf and I went together like pigs' feet and black-eyed peas - For a while, there was not one without the other, if you know what I mean. I was no Nicklaus or Woods, but I did make a hole-in-one twice at the famed Olympic Club Lake course, so I was surely going to miss the thrill of moments like that. I enjoyed entertaining my sons, friends, and the club members, especially with my steady game that allowed me to win more than my share of friendly wagers. I played the game with passion, and I was as happy on the course as anywhere else that I could imagine.

I am more likely remembered for the way I played the game than for the number of good rounds I had. I played golf a lot like Jackie Robinson, and my friend Willie Mays played baseball. I always dressed my absolute best and played to win – even if it meant taking the occasional risky shot. Even when the risks didn't pay off, they were fun to try, just like when

Mays attempted a daring basket catch or Robinson tried to steal home.

No one had ever done it like them, and no one ever will. That's the way I approached golf, as well as my career in business, technology, and politics, with love, passion, and that free-wheeling tenacity to go beyond what was expected of me. No one ever knew what I might try next, and I was often the first to do it. In my mind, nothing could stop me but myself. I suppose the love that I had for all my work and hobbies is one reason why I was able to compete for so long.

I was no longer playing golf, but I spent a considerable amount of time with my grandson Cameron, the son of Chris and my delightful daughter-in-law, Iris. Cameron is on the autism spectrum; therefore, it was important for me to learn more about autism and the understanding of inclusion. As a testament to, and example of the power of an autistic mind, my grandson Cameron is able to remember and immediately recite the teams and exact scores of every Prime-Time NFL football game played for the last 12 years! I gained a new understanding of the condition and the importance of giving youth on the spectrum a chance to succeed. Also, between 2010 and 2016, I enjoyed watching my other grandson, Connor, play baseball. He was a young star on the field, from Little League All-Stars to Majors Level Travel teams. I went to just about every game and in-town tournament in which Connor played. Most nights, after the games, I was hoarse from cheering so much for Connor and the team.

Yes, my journey started on an uneven playing field, considering the prejudice and segregation that I was subjected to from the moment I took my first breath, but I never let that stop me from being ambitious, self-motivated, and wanting to make a difference. Nothing could take that from me, not even racism. I thank my mother for instilling that in me. No matter what, I always had an unrelenting mindset. Even when things didn't look promising, I knew there was always another game, another competition, another door waiting to be opened. That door may not be easy to find, but the feeling that nothing could stop me kept me in the game, regardless of the adversities I faced. I know now that I was fortunate to have great women like my mother and my wonderful wife, Virginia, who always reminded me of that. I am also glad to see that the world is giving more opportunities to women to solve our global problems, utilizing their wisdom, intellect, and talents. It is absolutely the right time for us to move over, share the space, and watch as women take a chance to make the world a better place.

Recently, as I looked out over the hills from my current home, I thought about how proud I was when Barack Obama took his oath to become the 44th President of the United States, but more importantly, the first black man to be elected to that position. I can honestly say that I never thought it would happen, but when it did, I shed abundant tears of joy and was speechless for a day or so, which is not like me. I reacted no differently than most black Americans, as this was evidence that dreams can come true and that if we all join forces for the common good, all things are possible. It gave us hope, and hope is our friend. It was good for the economy right off the bat, as I had never seen so many black folks purchasing inaugural ball tuxedos and gowns in all my days. That was a great time for America.

While having lunch with my son, Rodney, I had a conversation about the major achievements of women, specifically, women of color. We talked about great women like the late NASA mathematician, Katherine Johnson, whose expertise was critical to the success of U.S. crewed spaceflights. We discussed Dr. Gladys West, a mathematician whose memoir, *It Began with A Dream*, tells how her calculations contributed to the development of the Global Positioning System (GPS) for the Navy. Those women are no longer hidden figures and are receiving the recognition that is long overdue. Many young women and girls are being inspired by the stories of Johnson and West, which shows the importance of representation to younger women. It's important for them to actually see someone who looks like them, who is working in a non-traditional field that they are interested in.

Rodney quickly remembered that I hired and mentored young women to work for us at Rod-L. He feels that there will be many more success stories of women making a difference in business, technology and communications, and media industries. We also talked about the women who have recently excelled in their respective fields and quickly rattled off names like the newly appointed

Ketanji Brown Jackson, the first black female Supreme Court Justice, Karine Jean-Pierre, the White House Press Secretary, and of course, Vice President Kamala Harris. They are all firsts in their roles and are more than qualified.

My sons and I have had recent phone conversations with women we know who have been successful in the Bay Area. Renel Brooks-Moon is the Public Address Game Announcer for the San Francisco Giants (MLB) baseball team. She is a leader in the organization and was the first woman to do it for the franchise when she was hired twenty-two years ago. Her parents, Nathaniel and Juanita Brooks, were educators in the Bay Area and good friends of mine back in the day. Nat, a big James Earl Jones type of guy, was the first black high school principal in San Francisco history. Renel says she has his voice, and I say she also has his welcoming smile. Although he is no longer with us, something tells me there are certain nights that he is somewhere looking down on his baby girl when she is booming out those familiar words, "Leading off for the Giants, number five..." We are so proud of Renel, who is currently one of only four women performing in such a role in major league baseball.

Shellye Archambeau is a longtime friend who I spoke to recently. She is the author of *Unapologetically Ambitious*, a former business executive, and a current board member of Verizon and other corporations. She had a cancer battle with her husband similar to what I went through with Virginia. Through our similar challenging times, we both learned the importance of embracing the support of friends and family. She has a great philosophy for success...among other things. She says, "No one succeeds without help and support from others. Don't be afraid to ask for support. Asking for help is not a sign of weakness, it's a sign of strength." I look forward to seeing more women, like Renel and Shellye, take their rightful seats at the table in every field.

This life has certainly been challenging for sure, but nothing worthwhile is easy. Some people ask me what my secret was and why I was so successful. First, I would not be who I am had it not been for my parents. I was raised to have big dreams and to believe in those dreams. My wife, Virginia, was also significant because she was always there every day, reminding me to be strong and stand up to all the challenges I faced. I am confident that those times of challenge brought out the best in me because I believed in myself, and my support system also believed in me as well... especially when I encountered those racially motivated challenges. To paraphrase my mother, "Don't let racism be an excuse for not being successful." She also said, "You must give respect to get respect." I listened, and I heard her loud and strong. I have lived by my mother's words from childhood, and I fully recommend them to you. Her little nuggets of wisdom gave me strength and confidence, and that's all I needed to go along with my work ethic and will to succeed.

I think of my mother and father often, and my brothers and sisters, not only for the good times we had as a family in Kinloch, despite our humble means, but I also think of how they always reminded me that I had high potential. In their unique ways, they kept me moving in the right direction and on the path to success.

Challenges, failures, and disappointments can either make or break you, and I was determined to succeed no matter the obstacles I encountered. If success was easy, everyone would have it. If you want it, you have to go and get it, no matter how often you hear that you will fail. That is what makes me feel so satisfied today. I would not feel this joy if everything I accomplished had been guaranteed. This joy is the culmination of all the wonderful moments of my life, coming together again, sort of full circle.

This past year, while completing my life story, I was recognized by the United Negro College Fund (UNCF) as their 2022 person of the year for my contributions to technology and the community in general. Also, a computer lab was opened in my honor, near my hometown of Kinloch, Missouri. The Roy Clay Sr. Computer Lab is located inside the 12th and Park Recreation Center in St. Louis. The services that it will provide for the young people of that community are immense. Services will include internet access, resume and career workshops, computer literacy/coding classes, video gaming, app development, Word, Excel, PowerPoint classes, and more. I was given special recognition by Congresswoman Cori Bush of St. Louis, which was also a special honor for me.

I am incredibly proud to have my name associated with a computer lab that will provide critical services to many deserving youths. Since I can no longer travel, I was not able to attend the opening ceremony for the laboratory. Fortunately, my nephew, Charles "Chuck" Henson (son of my sister Pauline), who still lives in St. Louis, was able to accept it on my behalf. The way Chuck stepped up to the plate for me was another example of how our family has always and will always support each other.

I am also proud and thankful to have been included in dozens of other articles and recognitions from organizations and publications, over the years, including Forbes Magazine, Black Enterprise Magazine, Intel Corporation, HP, Major Media Newspapers, and many other government entities, companies, and community-based organizations.

As I reflect on this life, I realize that it is the people that I have shared so much of my time with who have mattered more than any honor or accomplishment. I think about my brothers and sisters, my parents and my grandparents. In many ways, I am a little part of all of them. I am walking this journey without them now, and I hope I am making them proud.

I think of my teachers and how important they were in shaping my life. I think of Dr. Roy Johnson, who literally pieced me back together after that devastating football accident before I had even reached my teens. I think of the man I called Deacon, the Pool Hall owner, who was the first black businessman I ever knew. I will never forget the aroma of soul food that greeted me at the door of that old place, the crashing sound of the cue ball breaking the rack of balls to start each game, and the tense crap games behind closed doors in the back room. I mostly remember the wisdom and street smarts I gained from that experience.

I remember my first day at the newly integrated St. Louis University (SLU) and how I and a handful of other black students proved a lot of folks wrong by excelling in those hallowed classrooms and lecture halls against the odds. I can't forget and cannot stop smiling when I think of the white Jesuit Priest who was not only our professor but was also our poker-playing buddy on Saturday nights.

I also can't forget the times when I was denied work because of my race, but it never broke my spirit or hope, especially after marrying Virginia. I was teaching and holding other jobs, but I kept applying to McDonnell Aircraft and finally managed to land a position where I took advantage of the opportunity to sharpen my programming skills. I remember having a feeling that my experience there in programming would take me far, and it did – West Coast far, to be exact. A couple of years later, I worked at the Lawrence Livermore Laboratory in California, developing a computer program to track radiation fallout from atomic bombs. Next, I built mainframes and even a Fortran compiler for Control Data Corporation. That special project I worked on for Dr. Edward Teller at Livermore gave me credibility in the industry, and I was on my way from there.

There was my friend, David Jordan, who became a great friend and pushed me to excel at HP, where I met Dave Packard, who had already heard of my math and programming prowess at Livermore and CDC. Jordan had worked with me previously at CDC but was now at HP. I remember how my friend, Dave Jordan grilled me to prepare me for the interview with Packard. He has passed, but my sons and I are still friends with his daughter Phyllis, and son, Stanley Jordan, the renowned jazz guitarist. They are like family, and we see them whenever possible.

David Packard was one of the best leaders I ever worked with and a good man. I patterned my style of management after him and owe much of my success to Packard for giving me an opportunity to develop the computer division at HP. Before long, we had built the HP computer division, and the HP 2116A was the second commercial 16-bit computer. I still think about that day in 1966 when it was released, knowing that my team had taken a giant leap in changing the computing industry. Dave Packard came through with everything I asked for, and I stepped up to the challenge and provided him with a world-class product. We celebrated like it was the world series that week.

So many others come to mind, but more than anyone else, I will never forget Tom Perkins, one of my best friends. He took the time to learn about my life, and how different it was from his life. He got to know me as a person and understood how racism affected all of our lives. Tom and I helped each other understand racism and how to deal with it better. He also inspired me to be creative and use my imagination as the technology industry was ever-changing and in need of new companies with new ideas, which had a lot to do with me creating my company, ROD-L Electronics. Without Tom Perkins ' support and friendship, I would not have been a successful entrepreneur.

Virginia, while she could still travel, my sons and I had great times as a family throughout the 1990s, when I would meet up with a group of other black business professionals from around the country in New York each year. We would play golf at country clubs where some of the guys had memberships, including famous ones like Winged Foot and Westchester. During that week in New York, there was one night when we all dressed up, and I hosted a dinner for my group of friends and their spouses at the iconic 21 Club in Manhattan, which in its time, was like no other. It was a great week and an excellent opportunity to catch up with friends from around the country like Ron Gault, George Lewis, Darwin Davis, Cliff Gates, and several more. You know who you are. Thanks for those great memories.

I can never forget my Bay Area associates, such as my friends from the Green Meadow Area of Palo Alto, the OBGs, my golf buddies, my fellow Club members, and my staff at HP and at Rod-L. I think often about how they have always been there for me. Tony Davis, a good friend of Rodney and Chris, has spent a lot of time promoting my story whenever he's had an opportunity during the last few years. He and his wife Pauline also hosted a chitlin dinner at his house to celebrate my accomplishments. My mother always said one of the best things about getting old is that there is always someone cooking dinner for you. Mama was right. I will always remember those chitlins for sure. You have all played important roles in my life.

And lastly, to all the medical doctors, advisors, nurses, and technicians who were there for Virginia throughout her illness, and our friend, Reverend Floyd Thompkins, who came out of nowhere to help get us through our most difficult times. Thank you for helping my family.

In the spirit of strong family and the importance of family, my three sons are still in very close contact with all of my nieces and nephews. They have periodic "cousin" virtual get-togethers by way of the Zoom application. I have been in on some of those meetings, and they are hilarious, to say the least. Still, the love shared is very reassuring to me that those cousins and my sons will carry on our family values and traditions the way my parents, siblings, and I had envisioned. My sons and I live nearby and are very close to my brother, Haile's daughter, Andrea, and her husband, Colin. We still see each other on holidays and special occasions, and often for no reason other than simply being together.

While we are close to all of my nieces and nephews, we had the extra pleasure of traveling extensively with my niece, Denise. She is my brother Charles's daughter, and you have already heard my stories about how he protected me and was always there for me when I was a kid. Denise traveled with us to New York City, Europe, and Asia as we elaborated earlier. Charles passed away from Alzheimer's in 2018, one of the types of dementia that took all of my siblings. Thankfully, it has not affected me, but I am hoping that a cure will come about for this disease that has devastated so many families like mine. Denise wrote the letter below as a tribute to him. I want to share it with you as part of my story in remembrance of my big brother, Charles, to whom I give so much credit for making me the person that I am. He apparently did the same for his daughter Denise.

~Charles's Swan Song~

My dad, Charles Reed Clay, was a larger-than-life figure in my life. He was a World War II veteran. He was also the life of the party. He had an abundance of friends, a large and loving family, and was respected by those who knew him. He was caring and strong. He was disciplined and a free spirit. He was the smartest person I knew. He always had a rational answer to any question I posed and helped me solve many of life's mysteries.

My mother died young, from breast cancer, and my father no longer had a buffer between him and me, his 13-year-old daughter. He had to deal directly with me, the outspoken, independent, strong-willed image of himself. He didn't remarry until I was in my 30s. Little did I know, he wanted my approval of his chosen mate. Looking back, I took that as a sign of the respect he had for me.

My father had a great singing voice. I was told that he sang in the church choir as a boy, but I only heard him sing in the shower. He would bellow the songs of his youth. His favorite singers were Nat King Cole, Sam Cooke, and Lou Rawls. I would listen intently to the lyrics, not really understanding the message. I remember his two favorite go-to songs: "Straighten Up and Fly Right" by Nat King Cole made me laugh; "St. James Infirmary" by Lou Rawls made me sad. He thought Billie Holiday was one of the most beautiful and talented women in the world and Dinah

Washington's song, "What a Difference a Day Makes", tugged at his heartstrings.

The years passed, and I went on to college and moved away to attend graduate school. While we lived far apart, my relationship with my dad remained strong. We talked on the phone weekly and I was fortunate enough to be able to visit with him often and keep tabs on him as he aged. Eventually, Alzheimer's took my dad away from me, but it didn't take his song. Singing became the way he communicated. I would ask, "How are you feeling today, dad?". He would bellow.... "I'm feeling fine", in a strong baritone voice. As time passed, he would answer every question with a song. My dad lived with Alzheimer's for 12 years and died in 2018, at the age of 91. I miss him very much, but I still hear him in song. ~~ Denise Clay

When I think of my brother, which is almost every day, I go to this letter written by Denise, and it reminds me of those warm summer days and nights back in Kinloch, Missouri with my big brother Charles always there for me when times were tough. Indeed, I have very fond, warm thoughts of each one of mine and Virginia's siblings and all of our nieces and nephews.

We all have tough times, but it is the test of time that is the true mark of success and greatness. I hope my legacy is that I have made a positive difference in the world over a long period of time. I hope I have set the bar high and continue to do so for my sons and all those who may wish to follow me. Just remember, to be successful, you must stay true to your dreams, no matter where that vision takes you. The opportunity may only come once, so be prepared for it and be willing to work hard for it. It won't be easy, but it will be well worth it.

I did it and so can anyone else if they want it bad enough. In these words that paraphrase a quote by the great, Ralph Waldo Emerson, *I went where there was no path, and I left a new trail.* I hope my story has helped to give you some sense of direction if you are just starting out, or even if you have been walking alongside me for a while. One thing about life is that it goes on. So, I guess it is fair to say, "Come grow old with me, for the best is yet to come!" -Robert Frost.

It is my hope that this story will inspire some of you and help you find that road that may lead you towards being truly *Unstoppable*!

The Clay siblings. Left to Right: Haile, Imogene, Roy, Myrtle, Thaddeus, Pauline, Charles, Hope, Buddy.

This is me receiving an HP Legacy Award from then HP CEO Meg Whitman – an incredible honor

ACKNOWLEDGMENTS

This book is a gift to my family, friends and all others who appreciate true life stories of individuals who have overcome humble beginnings and achieved against the odds. I could not have published this memoir without the help and love of my three sons, Roy Clay, Jr, Rodney Clay, and Chris Clay (Project Director), tirelessly guiding me through the process and bringing the right team together to make it successful.

The writing team included my co-author, Marvin Jackson. He creatively brought my story to life, combining my words from notes, journals, articles, and many enjoyable conversations and interviews of acquaintances who have walked this journey with me. Erica Young brought an experienced literary eye to the team as our editor. I thank her for her professionalism and passion for the project. Our cover designer, Akapo Afeez played an immense role in providing the look and design that we desired from cover to cover.

So many family members and lifelong friends have contributed to me authoring this story that can now be passed down through generations to come. Those individuals include Denise Clay, Joyce Tinsley, Lori Tinsley, Chris Anthony Piganelli, Kara Anne Piganelli, Anthony Prior Piganelli, Virginia "Ginny" Prior, Shellye Archambeau, Jimmy Treybig, Gloria Young, Andrew Chamings, William "Bill" Green, Barry James, Phyllis Jordan, Stanley Jordan, Ken Coleman, Caretha Coleman, John W. Thompson, Butch Wing, Rev. Jesse Jackson, Eric Alperin and many, many others. I appreciate you all for your love and support.

Lastly, my story would not be possible without the lifelong love and support from the following family members who were all a part of my life. In many ways, a part of each of them will always be within me as I continue my journey.

Starting with my parents, Charles, and Emma Jean Clay. There would be no Roy Clay without you. My beloved wife, Virginia Clay who was everything to me, including the person who asked me years ago to author my story someday.

To my siblings, nieces, and nephews, and to Virginia's siblings and family. Thanks for always being there.

<u>My Siblings and family</u>
- o Pauline
  - ▪ Sons: Ronald, Aaron, Charles (Chuck)

- Daughter: Madye (Cissie)
  o Charles
    - Daughter: Denise
  o Thaddeus
    - Son: Thaddeus
  o William (Buddy)
    - Son: William (Buddy)
    - Daughters: Lisa, Quianna
  o Imogene
    - Sons: Eathel, Kaylon, Kendall (Kenny), Khris
  o Hope
    - Daughters: Sharmen, Lori
  o Myrtle
    - Daughter: Linda
  o Haile
    - Sons: Charles (Chuck), Haile
    - Daughter: Andrea

Virginia's Siblings and family

  o Louis (Lowell)
  o Robert (Bob)
    - Son: Robert Jr
  o Charles (Junebug)
    - Daughter: Phyllis
  o Violet (Lucky)

- Son: Ira (Shooney)
- Daughters: Terri, Toni, June, Joanne
  - Joyce
    - Daughters: Susan, Tina, Lori

Much appreciation to those of you who have read my story. My hope is that you have taken away something positive from my journey and enjoyed reading my story as much as I have enjoyed writing it.

ABOUT THE AUTHOR

Roy Clay Sr. was born in Kinloch, Missouri in 1929. After attending segregated public schools, he became one of the first African-Americans to graduate from Saint Louis University (SLU) with a B.S in mathematics in 1951. He relocated to California and began working as a programmer at Lawrence Livermore National Laboratory. His early work involved creating a radiation tracking system to study the aftermath of a nuclear explosion.

Hired by David Packard at Hewlett-Packard (HP) in 1965, Clay became a founding member of the Computer Division, where he was director of the team that developed the HP 2116A, Hewlett-Packard's first minicomputer. He established Roy L. Clay and Associates and worked closely with Tom Perkins (Kleiner Perkins) to become a contributor to the formation of Silicon Valley as we know it today. Clay founded Rod-L Electronics in 1977 and, as CEO, led it until 2015.

Mr. Clay was the first African American to join the City Council of Palo Alto, California and become Vice Mayor in 1976. He became the first African American member of the Olympic Club of San Francisco in 1989. He was inducted into the Silicon Valley Hall of Fame in 2003. Clay was married to the late Virginia Clay, and has three sons, Roy, Jr, Rodney, and Chris. He is known as the Godfather of Silicon Valley.

~unstoppableroyclay.com~

Made in USA - Kendallville, IN
28479_9780578269184
11.07.2023 1450